DUQUESNE STUDIES

Philosophical Series

25

THE IDEA

OF

DIALOGAL PHENOMENOLOGY

DUQUESNE STUDIES

Philosophical Series
25

THE IDEA
OF
DIALOGAL PHENOMENOLOGY

by
Stephan Strasser

Duquesne University Press, Pittsburgh, Pa.
Editions E. Nauwelaerts, Louvain

DUQUESNE STUDIES
Philosophical Series

Andrew G. van Melsen and Henry J. Koren, editors.

Volume One—*Andrew G. van Melsen,* From Atomos to Atom. Out of print.

Volume Two—*Andrew G. van Melsen,* The Philosophy of Nature. Pp. XII and 265. Third edition, fifth impression. Price: cloth $4.50. Published also in Italian, Dutch and Polish editions.

Volume Three—*P. Henry van Laer,* Philosophico-Scientific Problems. Out of print.

Volume Four—*Cajetan's* The Analogy of Names and The Concept of Being. Pp. X and 93. Second edition. Price: $2.25, cloth.

Volume Five—*Louis de Raeymaeker and others,* Truth and Freedom. Out of print.

Volume Six—*P. Henry van Laer,* The Philosophy of Science. Part One: Science in General. Pp. XVII and 164. Second edition. Price: cloth $3.75.

Volume Seven—*Stephan Strasser,* The Soul in Metaphysical and Empirical Psychology. Pp. X and 275. Third impression. Price: cloth $6.00. Published also in German, Dutch and French.

Volume Eight—*Albert Dondeyne,* Contemporary European Thought and Christian Faith. Pp. XI and 211. Third impression. Price: $5.75. Published also in French.

Volume Nine—*Maxwell J. Charlesworth,* Philosophy and Linguistic Analysis. Pp. XIII and 234. Second impression. Price: paper $4.75, cloth $5.50.

Volume Ten—*Remy C. Kwant,* Philosophy of Labor. Pp. XI and 163. Price: paper $4.50, cloth $5.25. Published also in Spanish.

Volume Eleven—*Remy C. Kwant,* Encounter. Pp. VIII and 85. Second impression. Price: cloth, $3.25. Published also in Dutch.

Volume Twelve—*William A. Luijpen,* Existential Phenomenology. Pp. 409. Revised Edition. Price: cloth $8.95. Published also in Dutch and Spanish. German edition in preparation.

Volume Thirteen—*Andrew G. van Melsen,* Science and Technology. Pp. X and 273. Price: paper $6.20, cloth $6.95. Published also in Dutch and German.

Library of Congress Catalog Card Number: 75-98549

© 1969, by DUQUESNE UNIVERSITY

Printed in the United States of America

Volume Fourteen—*P. Henry van Laer*, PHILOSOPHY OF SCIENCE. PART TWO: A STUDY OF THE DIVISION AND NATURE OF VARIOUS GROUPS OF SCIENCES. Pp. XIII and 342. Price: paper $5.75, cloth, $6.50.

Volume Fifteen—*Remy C. Kwant*, THE PHENOMENOLOGICAL PHILOSOPHY OF MERLEAU-PONTY. Pp. IX and 257. Price: paper $4.50, cloth $5.25. Published also in Dutch.

Volume Sixteen—*John A. Peters*, METAPHYSICS: A SYSTEMATIC SURVEY. Pp. XVIII and 529. Price: paper $9.00, cloth $9.75. Published also in Dutch.

Volume Seventeen—*William A. Luijpen*, PHENOMENOLOGY AND ATHEISM. Pp. XIV and 342. Second impression. Price: $4.25. Published also in Dutch.

Volume Eighteen—*Martin G. Plattel*, SOCIAL PHILOSOPHY. Pp. XI and 346. Price: paper $7.20, cloth $7.95. Published also in Dutch and German.

Volume Nineteen—*Andrew G. van Melsen*, EVOLUTION AND PHILOSOPHY. Pp. 208. Price: paper $4.75, cloth $5.50. Published also in Dutch and German.

Volume Twenty—*Remy C. Kwant*, FROM PHENOMENOLOGY TO METAPHYSICS. Pp. 247. Price: paper $7.20, cloth $7.95.

Volume Twenty-One—*Joseph J. Kockelmans*, PHENOMENOLOGY AND PHYSICAL SCIENCE. Pp. 208. Price: paper $6.20; cloth $6.95. Published also in Dutch.

Volume Twenty-Two—*William A. Luijpen*, PHENOMENOLOGY OF NATURAL LAW. Pp. 249. Price: paper $6.20; cloth $6.95. Published also in Dutch and Spanish.

Volume Twenty-Three—*Andrew G. van Melsen*, PHYSICAL SCIENCE AND ETHICS. Pp. 181. Price: paper $5.75, cloth $6.50. Published also in Dutch and German.

Volume Twenty-Four—*Emmanuel Levinas*, TOTALITY AND INFINITY. Pp. 300. Price: paper $8.75; cloth, $9.50. Published also in French and Dutch.

Volume Twenty-Five—*Stephan Strasser*, THE IDEA OF DIALOGAL PHENOMENOLOGY. P. xiii and 136. Price $5.95.

CONTENTS

SPECIAL REFERENCES AND TRANSLATIONS

Works by Husserl

Cart. Medit.: Cartesianische Meditationen und Pariser Vorträge, vol. I of *Husserliana,* The Hague, 1950. Translation by Dorion Cairns, *Cartesian Meditations, An Introduction to Phenomenology,* The Hague, 1960.

Ideen, vol. I: *Ideen zu einer reinen Phänomenologie und phänomenologischen Philosophie.* Erstes Buch, vol. III of *Husserliana,* The Hague, 1950. Translation by W. R. Boyce Gibson, *Ideas. General Introduction to Pure Phenomenology,* Allen and Unwin, London, 1931, Paperback ed., Collier Books, New York, 1962.

Ideen, vol. II: Zweites Buch, vol. IV of *Husserliana,* The Hague, 1952.

Ideen, vol. III: Drittes Buch, vol. V of *Husserliana,* The Hague, 1952.

Die Krise ...: Die Krise der europäischen Wissenschaften und die transzendentale Phänomenologie, vol. VI of *Husserliana,* The Hague, 1954.

Erste Philosophie (1923/4) Erster Teil, vol. VII of *Husserliana,* The Hague, 1956; *Zweiter Teil,* vol. VIII of *Husserliana,* The Hague, 1959.

Phänomenologische Psychologie, vol. IX of *Husserliana,* The Hague, 1962.

Zur Phänomenologie des inneren Zeitbewusztseins, vol. X of *Husserliana,* The Hague, 1966. Translation by Calvin O. Schrag, *The Phenomenology of Internal Time Consciousness,* Indiana University Press, n.d.

Analysen zur passiven Synthesis, vol. XI of *Husserliana,* The Hague, 1966.

Logische Untersuchungen, Teil I, Teil II/1 and II/2, 4th ed., Halle, 1928.

Erfahrung und Urteil, ed. by Ludwig Landgrebe, Hamburg, 1941.

Formale und transzendentale Logik, Halle, 1926.

Die Idee der Phänomenologie, The Hague, 1950. Translation by William P. Alston and George Nakhnikian, *The Idea of Phenomenology,* The Hague, 1964.

Works by others

Martin Heidegger, *Sein und Zeit,* 7th ed., Tübingen, 1953. Translation by John Macquarrie and Edward Robinson, *Being and Time,* New York, n.d.

Jean-Paul Sartre, *L'être et le néant,* 36th ed., Paris, 1950. Translation by Hazel E. Barnes, *Being and Nothingness,* New York, n.d.

Maurice Merleau-Ponty, *Phénoménologie de la perception,* Paris, 1945. Translation by Colin Smith, *Phenomenology of Perception,* New York, 1962.

PREFACE

In the past decades phenomenological philosophy has been exposed to criticism coming from many directions. Representatives of logical positivism, modern empiricism, linguistic analysis and the modern structuralist movement have not hesitated to address sharp reproaches to the spiritual heirs of Edmund Husserl. Yet, the convinced phenomenological philosopher will not be unduly impressed by these attacks. He knows that some of them are launched by non-philosophers and that the others come from philosophers whose concern is totally different from his own. He can safely disregard the former, while considering the latter's thought a valuable complement to his own. Generally speaking, he does not feel disturbed by the flood of anti-phenomenological criticism.

There is, however, something else which does cause uneasiness in the ranks of phenomenologists, viz., *the inability of Husserl's transcendental phenomenology to solve the problem of intersubjectivity*. The works of Max Scheler,[1] Adolf Reinach,[2] Wilhelm Schapp,[3] Martin Heidegger,[4] Karl Löwith,[5] Jean-Paul Sartre,[6] Maurice Merleau-Ponty[7] and Paul Ricoeur[8] bear witness to this concern. Their uneasiness can easily be understood. These authors are convinced that, if phenomenology proves unable to account for the social dimension of human existence, it cannot make any justifiable claim for a leading role in twentieth century philosophy. In this way one can understand why in the past few years various thinkers have made a concerted effort to reflect philosophically on the character of Husserl's major difficulty. We will limit ourselves here to naming René Toulemont,[9] Alfred Schütz,[10] Michael Theunissen[11] and R. F. Beerling.[12] Despite the differences in their styles of thinking and their starting points, the results of their

---

1. *Wesen und Formen der Sympathie*, 5th ed., Frankfurt a.M., 1948.
2. *Die apriorischen Grundlagen des bürgerlichen Rechtes*, Halle, 1913.
3. *In Geschichten verstrickt*, Hamburg, 1953; *Philosophie der Geschichten*, Leer, 1959.
4. *Sein und Zeit*, 7th impression, Tübingen, 1953.
5. *Das Individuum in der Rolle des Mitmenschen*, 2nd ed., Darmstadt, 1962.
6. *L'être et le Néant*, 36th ed., Paris, 1950.
7. *Phénoménologie de la Perception*, Paris, 1945.
8. "Sympathie et respect," *Revue de métaphysique et de morale*, 1954, pp. 380-397.
9. *L'essence de la société selon Husserl*, Paris, 1962.
10. *Collected papers*, 2 vols., The Hague, 1964.
11. *Der Andere*, Berlin, 1965.
12. *De transcendentale vreemdeling*, Hilversum, 1965.

inquiry are largely in agreement with respect to Husserl's philosophy of sociality. All these authors realize that something is lacking; they point to an essential deficiency. They could not avoid disclosing the sore spot disfiguring the body of transcendental phenomenology, which in other respects is so sound. This sore apparently is not disappearing spontaneously; it continues to fester and even threatens to poison the entire body of phenomenological philosophy.

Like many others, the author has lived for many years in the conviction that Husserl's failure to account for the social dimension of human existence was only a peripheral feature having no substantial importance. The edifice, of transcendental phenomenology was, so he thought, ingeniously planned and solidly executed. It merely was not finished in one respect. Husserl did not execute his program in this one respect, but, apart from that, the starting point and method of his philosophy were unassailable.

Yet, the author was struck by the strange fact that Husserl himself did not take such a light-hearted view. On the contrary, at the beginning of his fifth CARTESAN MEDITATION Husserl declared, with his characteristic inexorable honesty, that his transcendental idealism stands or falls with the possibility of solving the problem of intersubjectivity by means of the method of intentional analysis.[13] If, then, his attempt to do so must be considered a failure, this would appear to be an alarming sign. Does not this failure have far-reaching consequences? Doesn't it also throw a new light on the concepts of "world," "constitution," "intentionality" and "reduction"? Must we not proceed, in the *spirit* of Husserl, to a critical revision of the fundamental theses of transcendental phenomenology?

It is not in a casual and light-hearted fashion that the author made the decision to re-interpret the major themes of classical phenomenology. He has spent twenty-six years in the study of Husserl's philosophy. As a collaborator of the Husserl Archives of Louvain, transcribing, editing and interpreting Husserl's works, he has become intimately familiar with the thoughts of the founder of phenomenology. He has no illusions about the difficulties of his undertaking, and does not *a priori* exclude the possibility of mistakes and defects. There is one point, however, which he wishes to make in this matter, viz., he would like to be spared the would-be critic who, with a solemn voice and raised hand, wishes to remind him of Husserl's "little catechism" of phenomenology. Philosophically speaking, the author grew up with this "catechism" and, as a philosopher, he has outgrown it. The reasons why he no longer recognizes this "catechism" as a safe guideline for

---

13. *Cart. Medit.*, pp. 121-122.

contemporary phenomenological philosophy will be explained in this book. At the same time, however, the author will also point to the road by which the phenomenological movement can escape from its present impasse.

The content of this book was first presented, although not in the same complete form, as lectures at Duquesne University in Ocotober, 1968.

Stephan Strasser

Prior to the delivery of these lectures at Duquesne University a first translation of the text was made by Dr. Walter van de Putte. After the lectures, the expanded text was revised and finished by the undersigned and then submitted to the author for his approval. We owe an expression of thanks to Dr. James Erpenbeck for reading the text and suggesting certain changes to improve its readability.

Henry J. Koren

LECTURE ONE

A PHENOMENOLOGICAL EXAMINATION OF CONSCIENCE

1. Introduction: The Phenomenologist at the Crossroads

More than sixty years have elapsed since Husserl conceived his THE IDEA OF PHENOMENOLOGY (1907),[1] and when today we reflect upon the things to which this idea has given birth, we cannot fail to recognize two facts. Husserl's new philosophical reflection, which was first groping and hesitant, has managed to develop into a world-wide intellectual movement. It is an incontrovertible fact that the phenomenological movement has, in its various phases and forms,[2] fecundated and enriched the philosophy of the twentieth century.

It has fecundated Western philosophy by introducing new forms of thought, new methods and styles of thinking. It has also greatly enriched that philosophy by vastly expanding the field of philosophical reflection. Today all kinds of topics which formerly were largely disregarded now occupy a prominent place in philosophical studies; the earth and the landscape, building and dwelling, dancing and playing, laughing and crying, dread and nausea, etc. can no longer be considered unworthy of consideration or ridiculous. This expanded horizon of interest is due to the influence of phenomenology.

There is another side, however. We are obliged to recognize that the phenomenological movement has, so it seems, come to a standstill. Looking backwards, one can easily see that in the past phenomenology remained a movement because it generated a series of renewing impulses. It stayed alive by constantly rejuvenating itself.

In another study I have tried to show how that came to pass; how from being a "pure phenomenology" it became a "transcendental phenomenology," and how the latter, in its turn had to make room for "existential phenomenology."[3] It goes without saying that those metamorphoses did not occur without a struggle. One has merely to recall the strained relations between Husserl and Scheler, Heidegger's harsh critique of Husserl, the conflict between Sartre and Merleau-Ponty — these show that the evolution was not always a peaceful process. Yet, looking back to those clashes from a perspective of thirty, twenty or ten years, it is obvious that all those divergencies were expressions of life;

---

1. *Die Idee der Phänomenologie,* The Hague, 1950.
2. Cf. H. Spiegelberg, *The Phenomenological Movement,* 2 vols., 2nd ed., The Hague, 1965.
3. "Phenomenologies and Psychologies," *Review of Existential Psychology and Psychiatry,* vol. 5 (1965), pp. 80-105.

they witnessed to the passionate search for truth and to the philosophical struggle for life.

The thing that impresses the phenomenologist most when he considers the past decade is that there are no more conflicts, no more fundamental criticisms, no controversies about principles, but also no new philosophical impulses. Many people are convinced that the message of existential phenomenology, however valuable its contribution may have been, cannot be the last word of phenomenology and that, far from solving certain problems, existential phenomenology has not yet even posed them. At the same time, this feeling of discontent does not find expression in an outspoken, albeit constructive, critique.

Considerations of this kind give us the impression that the phenomenological movement of our time is faced with the need of making a decision. As always is the case, there is an easy way and a hard way of doing it, and the easy way could be taken in a twofold fashion.

First, one could "canonize" a particular form of phenomenology — for example, Husserl's transcendental phenomenology — proclaim it to be *the* phenomenology, and demand absolute orthodoxy from everyone who wishes to be called a phenomenologist. It is easy to see what the consequences of such an approach would be. A Husserlian scholasticism would then arise, a scholasticism in the bad sense of the term. Speaking more or less in the spirit of Wilhelm Wundt,[4] we could characterize it as follows. Such a scholasticism would desire to solve the most divergent problems by means of a uniform set of *a priori* accepted concepts; on the other hand, it would attach so much importance to traditional terms and concepts that it would not even question the basis for these terms and concepts. It is obvious that such an attitude would be in flagrant conflict with the spirit of Edmund Husserl.

In the second place, it is of course also possible to adopt a purely historical attitude toward the phenomenological movement. One would then devote oneself wholly to the task of editing and interpreting, to the hermeneutics of the texts written by phenomenological philosophers and to biographical research or historical monographs. This is, no doubt, an important task but it should not be considered the most important. We readily admit that such historical and critical text studies, thematic and hermeneutic examinations are useful and even necessary. But they are no substitute for original thinking about the problems in a spirit which is always ready to modify the conceptual apparatus if this is demanded by the adequate handling of the problems. If this spirit is lacking, then we would have here the beginning of the end of the phenomenological movement.

---

4. *Philosophische Studien,* vol. XIII, p. 345.

These two, then, are the relatively easy "solutions." To choose the hard way, one should of course have strong reasons. And if the phenomenologist wishes to convince himself that such reasons exist, he will have to perform an examination of his philosophical conscience. When he is in a situation of uncertainty, uneasiness and hesitation, it might be beneficial for him to reflect upon the original inspiration of phenomenological philosophizing. Such a reflection will of course include the task of interpretation and hermeneutics, but also the task of taking a position. And yet this position will not be something arbitrary, for it will be motivated, in both its positive and its negative aspects, by the past of the phenomenological movement. It will amount to a search for the principal sources of phenomenological inspiration.

Such an undertaking, moreover, deserves to be called truly phenomenological. For what is more in harmony with the *ethos* of Husserl, Scheler, Merleau-Ponty and the author of BEING AND TIME than the question about the foundation, the origin and the sources from which existential projects and intellectual achievements have come forth? After passing in review three generations of phenomenologists, studying their works and watching the many metamorphoses that have taken place in the phenomenological movement, the author can ask himself: What is *the* phenomenology? What is essential to it and what is not? What are the original driving forces and incentives of phenomenological philosophizing? What are its fundamental concerns?

A brief answer to those questions can only be given if we decide to simplify the range of problems somewhat. The historian of philosophy will notice that many particulars are absent from our discussion here. But with respect to the question with which we are concerned completeness is not necessary. That is why we feel justified in proceeding as follows. We will use Husserl's philosophy as a methodic guide line; only in passing and on occasion we will ask to what extent one can also find certain characteristics of Husserl's thought in other prominent phenomenologists, albeit in a modified form. At the same time, we will critically examine how the great concerns of phenomenology are related to one another; we will ask whether they are not at cross purposes, whether and how they can be realized.

Without claiming to be complete, the author believes that, from a hermeneutical viewpoint, four tendencies are typical of phenomenological thinking as such. We intend to characterize these fundamental tendencies here, compare them and, if necessary, subject them to criticism.

2. *The Intuitive and Anti-speculative Character of Phenomenology*

Phenomenology presents itself primarily as a philosophy of intuition

(*Anschauung*). Thus it appeared from the very start as a sharp reaction against the leading philosophical currents in Germany at the end of the nineteenth centruy, viz., positivism and neo-Kantianism. These two trends radically differed from each other in spirit; in fact, they were even antagonistic. Nevertheless, they agreed on one important point: both were oriented and attuned to science. Now, how does the scientist, especially one who is engaged in physical science, look upon intuition, perception and observation? It stands to reason that he cannot do without them, for perception gives him the indispensable starting point, the natural phenomenon. But for the scientist it is also incontrovertible that the perceived is *not* the reality. The real object is that which hides behind the smoke screen of sense impressions. In other words, reality, in the scientific sense of the term, is a construct which, starting from perceived data, is built up by means of mathematical operations of the mind. Hence intuition as such is not a source of reliable knowledge for the scientist.

This should be kept in mind if we wish to understand why in Husserl's work one of the constantly recurrent ideas is the assurance that what is seen in intuition is "immediately given," "itself present," "bodily present," the "thing itself." Even the imposing pyramid of abstraction which the modern scientist has erected is based on the firm ground of sense experience. It cannot exist without the foundation of the "everyday world." In a word, the phenomenon of the phenomenologist is the opposite of the phenomenon of the sciences. It is thanks to the phenomenon, the phenomenologist *proudly* tells us, that we grasp what-is itself; and it is upon this conviction that his entire philosophy is based.

This positive conviction of the phenomenologist goes hand in hand with the resolute rejection of a speculative and constructionist thinking that has lost contact with that which, itself, appears. Hence the well-known motto of the young Husserl: "Back to the things themselves" (*Zurück zu den Sachen selbst*). But in 1929, at the time when the founder of phenomenology professed a certain metaphysical conviction,[5] he added as a warning: "Actually, therefore, phenomenological explicitation is nothing like 'metaphysical construction' ... It stands in sharpest contrast to all that because it proceeds within the limits of pure intuition."[6] And elsewhere Husserl took a stand against "speculative constructs."[7]

5. *Cart. Medit.*, p. 166.

6. "Phänomenologische Auslegung ist also wirklich nichts dergleichen wie *metaphysische Konstruktion* ... Sie steht zu all dem im schärfsten Gegensatz durch ihr Verfahren im Rahmen reiner Intuition." *Ibid.*, p. 177 (tr. p. 150). Husserl's italics.

7. *Ideen*, vol. III, p. 141.

The question that arises spontaneously here is what Husserl means by "speculative," for this philosophical term has various meanings. André Lalande defines two senses of the term "speculation" in his dictionary: "A. Thought which has no other object than that of knowing. B. Hence, but now with a pejorative implication, an abstract and arbitrary construction that cannot be verified and that has a doubtful value."[8] Thus, according to Lalande, the characteristics of "speculation" in the second sense are as follows. This kind of speculative thinking does not start from a real experience but from a theoretical construct. It rests on presuppositions that are more or less arbitrary; hence they cannot be tested for their truth-value. Perhaps we could also say — somewhat in line with Karl Jaspers — that speculative thinking, while carrying out its sovereign movement of thought, does not let itself be guided by any object as its norm.

If we start from that pejorative meaning of the term — and this meaning was the vogue in Husserl's time — we must say that phenomenological thought is exactly the opposite of speculative thought. For the phenomenologist starts from a matter that is perceived, whether it be a thing, a social relationship, or a phenomenon in consciousness. And he tries to discover the "rule structure" which the matter in question prescribes to the knower. That is, he lets himself be ruled, as by a norm, by what he perceives, by what he imagines or what he thinks. Husserl explicitly declares that no intellect, not even the divine Spirit, can free itself from the rules which the "matter as matter" prescribes to it.[10] All the other qualities expected of a phenomenologist, such as fidelity, simplicity and the self-control that prevents him from launching himself into "metaphysical adventures," flow from his submission to that which presents itself, to that which itself appears.

3. Phenomenology as Reductive-dialectical Philosophy

Our claim regarding the intuitive character of phenomenology is not likely to meet much objection. After all, it has been made, if not explicitly then at least implicitly, by such prominent phenomenologists as Scheler, Heidegger,[11] Sartre and Merleau-Ponty. For these philosophers would not make so much use of description if they did not

---

8. "A. Pensée n'ayant d'autre objet que de connaître ... B. Par suite, avec un import péjoratif, construction abstraite et arbitraire qu'on ne saurait vérifier et dont la valeur est douteuse." *Vocabulaire technique et critique de la philosophie,* Paris, 7th ed., 1956, p. 1019.

9. *Philosophie,* vol. 3, *Metaphysik,* Berlin, 1932, p. 135.

10. *Ideen,* vol. I, p. 101.

11. Here we speak of Heidegger only as the author of *Sein und Zeit.*

feel confident that they could penetrate to the heart of the matter through intuitive experience.

When, however, we mention the dialectical-reductive character as the second characteristic of phenomenology, this claim, on the contrary, will cause astonishment. Yet, it is certain that phenomenology is different from every form of realism, impressionism and common sense philosophy precisely by its dialectical-reductive character.

Let us start from the expression we have just used and ask ourselves how the phenomenologist proceeds in order to "penetrate to the heart of the matter." With respect to Husserl, three different answers must be given to that question, but these answers have a dialectical relationship to one another.

The first thing the phenomenologist must do is indeed to "perceive" and "describe," and this task is, of course, in the first instance concerned with concrete and individual reality. Such a perception of reality can easily be changed into an intuition of the nature of the reality in question.[12] What is "perceived" is, for example, a sound I hear or a thing I see. In the second instance the object of intuition is the essence of "sound" in general or the *eidos* of the "spatially extended thing" in general. It is in this sense that Husserl says: "Immediate seeing, not merely the sensory seeing of experience, but seeing in general as primordial dator consciousness of any kind whatsoever, is the ultimate source of justification for all rational assertions.[13] And in another context Husserl calls the confidence placed in perceived reality the "primordial faith" (*Urdoxa*), the foundation upon which all abstraction, including that of science, rests.[14]

Thanks to a radical change in our cognitive attitude, viz., the phenomenological reduction, we realize that this external reality and its essential characteristics cannot be the foundation sought by the philosopher. The "heart of the matter" is not this reality, but it is the achievement of consciousness by means of which that reality becomes real for me. The "primordial faith" is thus shaken up. Something else now seems to be more fundamental: "It is absolutely certain to us that being-an-object is, phenomenologically speaking, based on certain acts in which something appears, or is thought of, as an object."[15] In other words,

---

12. *Ideen,* vol. 1, pp. 13 f.
13. "Das *unmittelbare Sehen (noein),* nicht blosz das sinnlich erfahrende Sehen sondern *Sehen überhaupt als originär gebendes Bewusztsein* welcher Art immer, ist die letzte Rechtsquelle vernünftiger Behauptungen." *Ideen,* vol. I, p. 44; transl. pp. 75 f.
14. *Ideen,* vol. I, p. 260.
15. "Als das Allersicherste gilt [uns] dasz das Gegenstand-sein, phänomenologisch gesprochen, in gewissen Acten liegt, in welchen etwas als Gegenstand erscheint oder gedacht ist." *Logische Untersuchungen,* vol. II/1, p. 362.

the firm ground that is now discovered is formed by consciousness conceived phenomenologically. This ground Husserl characterizes as "the epistemologically first sphere of absolute certainty."[16]

This is not the last word, however. For psychical interiority, albeit freed from all naturalistic misconceptions, is not yet transcendental consciousness, that is, the transcendental subjectivity which constitutes in itself, in its active life, all reality, including also psychical reality. Now *this* conscious life appears to be the "heart of the matter," the unshakable foundation of all apodictic knowledge. The important thing that is now perceived is the transcendental stream of consciousness as it appears to itself thanks to transcendental self-experience.

The road that leads to this realm of all constitutive life is no longer phenomenological reflection but an action that is much more powerful, viz., the transcendental-phenomenological reduction. Hence there is also a change in the aim pursued by the phenomenologist. As a transcendental phenomenologist he has as his task "to point out and show this subjectivity in its performance, in its ... transcendental ... conscious life, in the certain ways in which it 'brings about' in itself the world as meaning of being. It is not his task to invent nor mythically to construct.[17]

Even this is not all. The concrete "stream of consciousness" or thought cannot be perceived as such; it cannot be "shown" or described. Husserl affirms this very clearly in his INAUGURAL LECTURE AT FREIBURG. The actual consciousness resembles the stream of Heraclitus; its "waves" cannot be grasped because of their flowing and unsteady character. Only the general structure of consciousness, only its *a priori* form can be revealed. That is why phenomenology is not a psychology, not even an introspective psychology of consciousness. Its relationship with psychology is more like that of geometry with geography.[18] With respect to this point one can, of course, ask oneself to what extent geometric entities of reason are perceivable objects, whether a general structure is identical with the "self-given" and whether an *a priori* conformity with law can be called "the matter itself."

One thing should be clear from this brief, and perhaps even scanty, sketch.[19] Husserl's phenomenology presents itself as a philosophy of intuition. But at the same time something strange happens. The "what" of intuition seems again and again to be less interesting to him than the "by what"; the *quod* (what) inspires less interest than the *quo* (by

---

16. *Ibid.,* p. 335.
17. *Die Krise der europäischen Wissenschaften . . .* , p. 156.
18. *Die reine Phänomenologie, ihr Forschungsgebeit und ihre Methode,* Manuscript F I 13 of 1917. Cf. also *Cart. Medit.,* p. 36 and *Ideen,* vol. I, p. 172.
19. Compare this sketch with Husserl's text in *Cart. Medit.,* §15, pp. 72-73.

what). Everything which at the start seems to be simply "given" subsequently blossoms out as the product of another something "given" on the basis of a new reductive reflection, while this "other" is, in its turn, relativized in the course of another and even more radical reduction.

The reductive ethos of Husserl's phenomenology seems to be strangely in conflict with the intuitive ethos. Fundamentally, however, this is not surprising. For the character and sequence of the reductions and the fact that they have their foundation in one another manifest an evident dialectical character.[20] Truly, it must be said that this dialectic is characteristic of Husserl's philosophy.[21]

It is well known that intuition plays only a small role within a typically dialectical way of thinking. One has only to think here of Fichte and Hegel as examples. Intuition does indeed constitute the starting point of their reflection, but this starting point is quickly relativized and "sub-lated." Husserl made heroic efforts to unite the two ways of thinking— intuitive and dialectic thinking— into a grand synthesis. But it is not at all certain that he has been successful. When one enters more deeply into his work, one becomes aware of certain difficulties. These we must now consider here.

Intuition, according to Husserl, is tantamount to the ultimate "satisfaction" of the mind that strives for insight. Consciousness, being now able to contemplate its object adequately, is satisfied, at peace, it is at rest. Thanks to intuition, "signitive" knowledge is changed into "consciousness of fulfillment" (*Erfüllungsbewusztsein*). From being an empty anticipation it becomes the grasping of a given content. Thanks to intuition, what was first a consciousness of a vague horizon becomes the contemplation of "the matter itself." In other words, in Husserl's philosophy intuition plays a role that is similar to that of "quieting" (*quietatio*) in the scholastic theory of the human act (*actus humanus*). Well known also is Husserl's careful, exact and loving description of

---

20. It is true that Husserl did not use the term "dialectics," but he was familiar with the essence of dialectic thinking. Other prominent phenomenologists also are no strangers to it. It may suffice to refer here to the dialectic of the concepts "even a phenomenon" and "merely a phenomenon" in Heidegger's *Sein und Zeit* (pp. 28-30), to the dialectic structure of the argumentation in several chapters of Merleau-Ponty's *Phénoménologie de la perception* and to the leading ideas in Sartre's *L'être et le Néant*, which remind us of Hegel. Moreover, it is no coincidence that Merleau-Ponty sees Hegel, Kierkegaard and Marx as forerunners of phenomenology (*Phénoménologie de la Perception*, Avant Propos, p. II), and that De Waelhens extensively compares Husserl with Hegel (*Existence et signification*, Louvain, 1958, pp. 7-29).

21. Cf. S. Strasser, "Intuition und Dialektik in der Philosophie Edmund Husserls," *Edmund Husserl, 1859-1959*, The Hague, 1959, pp. 148-153.

that which, according to him, is the primary object of perceiving intuition, viz., the spatially extended thing.

Nevertheless, the reductive ethos of transcendental phenomenology demands that we not surrender ourselves to the spectacle of things. For this would mean giving in to the "natural attitude." The naiveté of lingering, in astonishment and admiration, with things, living beings and persons — in short, with the world — needs to be overcome by the phenomenological reduction. Through an act of asceticism we discover an entrance to a new realm, the realm of psychical consciousness with its meaningful *noeses* and *noemata*. This psychism could also be a region in which we could more deeply immerse ourselves through our acts of internal contemplation. Yet, we must once again tear ourselves away from it, for the being of that "inner world" is, we are told, just as much based on the achievements of transcendental subjectivity as is the being of the "external world." But transcendental self-experience as such cannot be described; all we can do is determine its *a priori* structures.

Once again, then, the phenomenologist who expects finally to satisfy his desire for insight through intuition meets with disappointment. He is not unlike Sancho Panza, the man who was called to be king in Cervantes' famous story: Sancho was offered the most appetizing foods, but as soon as he wished to eat of them, the royal physician came foreward, declaring that the dishes were unhealthy and ordering that they be taken away.

The inner tension which permeates Husserl's thought manifests itself clearly in the idea of the "disinterested observer."[22] Husserl, as is well known, compares the Ego that remains after the completion of the transcendental-phenomenological reduction to an onlooker who attentively watches the world but has no interest in it at all. Why is the idea of the "disinterested observer" so unsatisfactory? A follower of existential phenomenology, such as Merleau-Ponty, would remark that such an observer would have to survey the whole world without any personal point of view, without any perspective, any horizon; and he would add that the postulate of such an "all-surveying look" is contrary to all our perceptive experience. The imaginary observer would float above the world; he would not live in it.

Perhaps we must even go further. In our opinion it is clear that the concept of a "disinterested observer" contains a self-contradiction. One who carefully observes something is, by that very fact, interested in it. Interest is, in fact, characteristic of an observer as an observer. One can refer here to a hunter who watches an approaching deer, a mother

---

22. *Cart. Medit.*, § 15, p. 72.

who keeps an eye on the behavior of her child, or to a spectator who watches a game in the World Series. The scientific observer, too, looks with intense attention at something that raises his professional interest. Generally speaking, we do not even notice things that do not interest us at all.

The contradiction in question can be detected even in Husserl's own text. We are told, on the one hand, that the transcendental observer "does not occupy himself" with the world and worldly things, that is, he distances himself from them, he maintains no active relations with them. On the other hand, the observer must "see" and even "adequately describe" the world.[23] To look at something with attention and adequately describe it are surely active contributions requiring a certain effort; moreover, again, we cannot avoid asking ourselves why an Ego would watch a world in which it has no interest whatsoever.

Let us now return to our starting point and ask why we ought to tear ourselves away from worldly things if they are so attractive, so worthwhile looking at, so full of rich food for our contemplation. Why should we "bracket the world," give it an "index of nothingness," "suspend the thesis" of its existence, when the world is the field in which we can make perceptive explorations? To use again the comparison mentioned above, who is like the physician who warned Sancho Panza that the food was not wholesome and ordered it to be taken away? Husserl does not leave us in uncertainty. The inexorable physician is the philosopher himself who permits only apodictically certain insights to be used as the valid foundation of philosophical and scientific understanding. It is the search for the unshakable ground of all knowledge that prevents Husserl from naively surrendering to the spectacle of the world. "The quest for a rigorous science of philosophy"[24] is the driving force of Husserl's entire dialectic. What we have called "the heart of the matter" is for Husserl identical with matter which is free from every imaginable doubt. This is evident from Husserl's entire work.

The two tendencies — confidence in what is given and the Cartesian search for an apodictically certain knowledge — did not reach a perfect balance in Husserl's philosophy. Alphonse de Waelhens has pointed this out very clearly.[25] We hear, on the one hand, that "the immediate seeing, not merely the sensory seeing of experience, but seeing in general as primordial dator consciousness of any kind what-

---

23. *Ibid.*

24. Cf. Marvin Farber, *The Foundation of Phenomenology. Edmund Husserl and the Quest for a Rigorous Science of Philosophy,* Cambridge, Mass., 1943.

25. *Phénoménologie et vérité,* Paris, 1953.

soever is the ultimate source of justification for all rational assertions."
On the other hand, we are told with respect to the existence of the
world that, "not only can a particular experienced thing suffer deval-
uation as an illusion of the senses; the whole unitarily surveyable
nexus, experienced throughout a period of time, can prove to be an
illusion, a coherent dream."[26]

There is more involved here than a logical inconsistency. The source of
the difficulty lies deeper. When we ask why Husserl's dialectic is so
little in harmony with his doctrine about intuition, the answer is:
because his dialectic does not flow from the intuition. On the contrary.
The intuitive ethos demands that we accept with perfect seriousness that
which presents itself to us. The spatially extended thing — Husserl
once spent five semester hours on its description[27] — is a most real
being. That which presents itself to our perception is an object of our
"primordial faith"; and the world which is the field of our actual and
possible experiences, of itself does not tell us that it could ever prove
to be a mere dream phenomenon. It is the Cartesian philosopher, the
epistemologist, the founder of a rigorously scientific philosophy who
demands of us that we consider as mere phenomenon that which for us
was self-evident reality; he demands that we have distrust where we
first had trust, and even that by our own power we cause our "primordial faith" to waver.

We can also compare Husserl in this matter with the dialectic used
by Hegel in his PHENOMENOLOGY OF THE MIND, for this comparison
leads to interesting discoveries. In Hegel, too, there is repeatedly question of new acts of "bracketing" things; but here the need to do this
flows from the experiences themselves which consciousness has. For
example, "sense certainty" (sinnliche Gewiszheit) itself comes to the
discovery that it is not a "knowing" (Wissen). Perception is at a complete loss; it must rise higher to the unconditional general knowing of
the mind.[28] In short, the two characters which we have brought to the
stage in connection with Husserl's reduction — Sancho Panza and the
physician — are, for Hegel, one person, viz., the diner himself, who
discovers that some foods are not healthy and who is therefore forced
to change his habits of eating.

---

26. "Nicht nur dasz Einzelerfahrenes die Entwertung als Sinnenschein erleiden
kann, auch der jeweils ganze, einheitlich überschaubare Erfahrungszusammen-
hangender kann sich als Schein erweisen under dem Titel zusammenhangender
Traum." Cart. Medit., p. 57 (transl. p. 17).
27. Hauptstücke aus der Phänomenologie der Vernunft, Manuscript F I 13
of 1907.
28. Phänomenologie des Geistes, ed. by Lasson, pp. 74, 87.

Should we not see in this a useful hint for the phenomenological philosopher?

4. Phenomenology as Philosophy of Intentionality

The third characteristic of phenomenological philosophy is the idea of intentionality. This is readily admitted by all. For Husserl characterizes intentionality "as a comprehensive title of general phenomenological structures" and he calls intentionality the "chief theme of phenomenology."[29] Other phenomenologists have taken over the idea of intentionality, albeit under different names and with significant modifications.

It is well known that Husserl first discovered the referential character of consciousness in connection with the phenomenon of language. A new era in European thought dawned when he declared that "our interest, our intention, that which we mean (as speaking) ... turns solely to the matter that is meant in an act of giving meaning."[30] Other writers[31] have carefully examined how Husserl in this respect modified the idea of intentionality that was proposed by Brentano. The matter intentionally aimed at by consciousness is, according to Husserl, appreciated and conceived in a special way; it is endowed with a certain meaning. For example, we do not hear acoustic stimuli, but we hear the twitter of a bird. Thus intentionality always has an objectifying character. From this it follows that to be intended, to be an object of my perception, my imagination, thought or desire and to be-for-me are, for Husserl, different ways of expressing one and the same thing.

The idea of intentionality underwent, of course, a certain change when Husserl passed from "pure phenomenology" to "transcendental phenomenology." At an earlier time he had confined himself to determining correlative relationships, with the understanding that to perception there *corresponded* the perceived, to striving that which is striven for, to appreciating that which is appreciated — more generally expressed, the meaningful *noema* corresponded to the meaninggiving *noesis*. Later, however, he spoke of "constituting" and "being constituted." That which is thought of, the *cogitatum*, arises from the

---

29. "... als einen umfassenden Titel durchgehender phänomenologischer Strukturen ... "; "... das phänomenologische Hauptthema ... "; *Ideen,* vol. I, pp. 203, 204.

30. "Unser Interesse, unsere Intention, unser vermeinen (als Sprechende) ... geht ausschlieszlich auf die in sinngebenden Akt gemeinte Sache." *Log. Unters.,* vol. II/1, p. 40.

31. Cf., e.g., Th. de Boer, *De ontwikkeling in het denken van Husserl,* Assen, 1966.

cogito; the intentional act or function is an act or function which *brings about* that which is intended, in a manner that has to be determined separately for each ontological region. We will not enter here into a discussion of the much-debated problem of that "constitution."

Another question, more simple but also more fundamentally important, demands our attention. Husserl describes intentionality as a "turning to,"[32] "being involved in,"[33] and "being orientated to."[34] Let us note at once that he uses these expressions even after the transcendental-phenomenological reduction has been made. But Husserl does not explain how it happens that consciousness tends or directs itself to something. Why does consciousness turn to something which it is not (i.e., not yet or no longer)? Where, as Sartre, remarks, does that little word "not" come from? The problem is not solved by conceiving intentionality as a giving of meaning. On the contrary, if consciousness itself is the source of all conceivable meaning, why does it "aim" at that which is less meaningful? Why does it center into a relation with that which is meaningless?

The same difficulty can also be approached from a different standpoint. We will make use here of a reflection of De Waelhens[36] which, however, we will radicalize. One can say with De Waelhens and most existential phenomenologists that consciousness is essentially a "going out of oneself" and "ex-istence."[37] If so, the nature of consciousness is "openness."[38] Then we fully understand expressions such as "turning," "directing itself to" and "referring to." But it is then impossible to hold, at the same time, that consciousness "when considered in its purity has to be looked upon as a coherence of being that is closed upon itself . . ., in which nothing can penetrate and from which nothing can slip out."[39] And if we say it anyhow, we expose ourselves to the deserved reproach of "essential ambiguity."[40]

On the other hand, the existential-phenomenological view cannot be considered the last word. For once again, why is man's existence essentially a "standing out toward" something that man is not not?

---

32. *Ideen,* vol. I, pp. 77, 82.
33. *Ibid.,* p. 80.
34. *Ibid.,* pp. 81, 204.
35. *L'être et le Néant,* pp. 37-113.
36. "L'idée phénoménologique d'intentionnalité," *Husserl et la pensée moderne,* The Hague, 1959, pp. 115-142.
37. *Ibid.,* pp. 119, 133.
38. *Ibid.*
39. "In Reinheit betrachtet als ein für sich geschlossener Seinszusammenhang zu gelten hat . . . in den nichts hineindringen und aus dem nichts entschlüpfen kan." *Ideen,* vol. I, p. 117.
40. De Waelhens, *op.cit.,* pp. 121, 135.

Or to use a different expression, if man is a "natural light," why does
he enter into darkness? If he, and he alone, is the bearer of any possible meaning, why does he "aim" at that which is meaningless? An
answer must be given to this question, and answer which makes use of
all the valuable contributions of existential phenomenology but which,
at the same time, completes them.

5. Phenomenology as Philosophy of Genesis

The fourth characteristic of phenomenology consists, in our opinion,
in this that it is a philosophy which asks the question concerning the
ground and the coming-to-be of the phenomenon. It essentially desires
to clarify the origin of the phenomena. In this sense we can say that it
is a philosophy with a genetic orientation. This it has been from the
very start. As early as 1891, in his PHILOSOPHY OF ARITHMETIC, Husserl
examined the foundation on which rest notions such as unity, multi-
plicity and number. The older Husserl spoke of "universal genesis"[41]
and of intentional references to a "history" of phenomena.[42]

Something similar can be said with respect to other great phenomenologists. Max Scheler tries to explain the origin of value consciousness and of moral consciousness.[43] We can see from numerous titles of
Martin Heidegger's works how great his interest is in the question of
the "ground," the "origin" of things. Jean-Paul Sartre tries to find the
origin of negation.[44] Maurice Merleau-Ponty considers it his principal
task to shed light on the "conditions of reason," that is, the pre-rational
dimension which makes man's reason possible.

Today's phenomenologists also show great interest in the genesis of
phenomena. This is evident whenever they enter into discussions with
representatives of other contemporary trends of thought. The logical
positivists, for example, with great acumen examine the structure of
particular scientific propositions. The linguistic analysts microscopically
examine particular types of linguistic acts. But the phenomenologists
claim the right to ask how scientific judgments and, in general, language expressions arise. This interest of the phenomenologist, which is
so different from that of others, is a source of frequent misunderstanding.

But let us return to Husserl. How, according to him, should the
origin and the coming-to-be of phenomena be investigated? The funda-

---

41. *Cart. Medit.,* p. 170.
42. *Ibid.,* p. 113.
43. *Der Formalismus . . . ,* 3rd ed., 1927, pp. 163 ff. Cf. Manfred S. Frings,
Max Scheler, Pittsburgh, 1965, pp. 70 f.
44. *L'être et le néant,* passim.

mental answers is: by means of intentional analysis. The starting point and guide-line for this examination is the intentional object. The question asked is, to what intentional acts and functions does a being owe its being-an-object-for-me? For example, to what acts of perception, remembrance and emotional expectation based on them, does the object's validity as a being correspond; for instance, an object such as a "letter from my wife"? This, then, is what should be discovered by means of an intentional analysis.

In transcendental phenomenology a similar method is used to investigate the process of "constituting" worldly beings in transcendental consciousness. From which *cogito*, from which series of interconnected and mutually dependent *cogito's* did that *cogitatum* come forth? What structure must these *cogito's* possess so that they may be able to constitute objects of this or that kind? That is the question raised within the framework of a transcendental view. It was in this way that Husserl hoped to draw up a universal theory of the process of "transcendental constitution."[45]

The transcendental object, then, is in every case the starting point and contains the necessary directives to lead us back to its origin. But how do we proceed on this way? Here, too, Husserl does not leave us in uncertainty. "Necessarily the point of departure is the object given 'straightforwardly' at the particular time. From it reflection goes back to the mode of consciousness at that time and to the potential ways of consciousness included horizonally in that mode, and then to those in which the object might be otherwise intended as the same."[46]

Let us explain this by means of an example. While perceiving, I live "with" the perceived; for example, my bookcase. Through an act of reflection I recover a series of acts of perception and syntheses of perceptions to which the bookcase owes its being-real-for-me. Moreover, I see that bookcase only from one side, the side that faces me. To the "horizon" of my perceiving consciousness belongs the vague awareness of the fact that the thing has also a back. Through a new reflection I become conscious of the fact that in principle I have the ability to walk around the bookcase and look at its back. I have thereby "made clear" the possibility which was implied in the horizon —

---

45. *Cart Medit.*, pp. 87-91.
46. "Der Ausgang ist ja notwendig der jeweils geradehin gegebene Gegenstand, von dem aus die *Reflexion* zurückgeht auf die jeweilige Bewusztseinsweise und auf die in dieser horizontmäszig beschlossenen, potentiellen Bewusztseinsweisen, dann au diejenigen, in denen er sonst als derselbe bewuszt sein könnte." *Ibid.*, p. 87 (Husserl's italics). Cf. also, e.g., *Ideen*, vol. I, pp. 177 ff.

as a horizon of perception and a practical horizon.[47] All this sounds very plausible.

But is it really plausible? Is it true that it belongs to the *essence* of the perception of a thing that the perceiving subject has the ability to change his place and look at the thing from all sides? Is the body of the perceiving subject essentially "a freely moved whole of sense organs"?[48] What about a small child, for example, whose sense powers are already fully developed but who is not yet able to walk? Does he, too, possess "in principle" the ability to look at the other side of every thing by taking up a different position? Evidently not. The small child looks at the bookcase just as we look at the moon. Hence a prominent child psychologist rightly declares that the ability to walk is an important step in the development of man on the road to independence and, of course, also toward the independent reconnoitering of spatially extended reality.

Our objection seems, at first sight, not to be of considerable importance. There cannot be any doubt as to what Husserl would have answered to it. Being a child, he would have said, means not yet to possess a normal body, and in this sense the child is still "anomalous." Husserl never denied that anomalies result in deviating ways of constituting reality. He even wrote extensively on this topic.[50]

This answer, however, does not yet remove all difficulties. Two questions impose themselves here. How does the transcendental phenomenologist know what is normal? And, how does he know that anomalies exist?

Let us provisionally leave the first question out of consideration, although it is important. Let us accept that being a child is not a way of being-man but a deviation from the human norm, an anomaly. It is then an anomaly that everyone of us has gone through; each one of us experienced for some time the spatial world around him in a way that is typical for a being who cannot freely move about. But even if with the utmost attention we reflect upon our childhood years, this reflection will not teach us anything about the style of our perceptive life of those early years. We are simply incapable of representing to ourselves that father's bookcase did not have a back for us. Neither can we recall the feelings of inferiority that arose because we felt helpless and had to rely on others to move from place to place. And yet it

---

47. *Ideen,* vol. I, p. 84.
48. "Frei bewegtes Ganzes der Sinnesorgane." *Ideen,* vol. II, p. 56.
49. H. Remplein, *Die seelische Entwicklung des Menschen im Kindes- und Jugendalter,* 14th impression, Munich, 1966, p. 191.
50. *Ideen,* vol. II, pp. 68 f. and in many unpublished manuscripts.

is possible that these and other childhood experiences are important for our intentional life of today. It is possible that they form a stratum that is now buried but that, nevertheless, is the foundation upon which other structures rest.

Leaving out the imagery, what does it mean when we say that a child's experience or a stratum of such experiences are "buried"? The expression obviously does not refer to a case of simply "forgetting" those experiences, for what we have forgotten is in principle subject to recall. But our relations to certain childhood experiences differ totally from, for example, the relation to a name which we are unable to recall at a particular moment. Perhaps we could say that the fact that childhood experiences are "buried" means that we have outgrown them. A new life, another kind of life has been formed and has taken the place of the earlier life.

That is not all, however. That growing and outgrowing was perhaps possible only because a certain style of experiencing the world was given up, because certain structures of a child's consciousness disintegrated and were replaced by others. Perhaps a "productive disintegration"[51] was needed for the birth of a mature consciousness. If this is true, then development is impossible without change; and change then also means a change of structures. Our perceptive life as adults differs structurally from the perceptive life of a child.[52] Yet it could be true that our present style of perceiving became possible only by the fact that we first perceived things in a way that was essentially different.

Let us now return to the question with which we began. How does the philosopher know that there are anomalies? How does he know that he himself has been subject to an anomaly? How does he know that his conscious life formerly presented other structures? Negatively we can say that he never knows this by means of a reflection. No reflection teaches me what my experiences were just after I was born. No reflection enables me to foretell how my visible perception will change if I take the santonin drug.[52] No imagination tells me how the world would appear to me if I were to become blind.[54] The positive answer, on the other hand, would be: that there are anomalies, what changes in structure result from them, and how they influence the "constitution" of the world, are things which the philosopher knows only through certain *experiences* and, in the first place, through certain experiences of *other people*.

---

51. Cf. H. C. Rümke, *Ontwikkelingspsychologie en psychotherapie*, Amsterdam, p. 10; *Levenstijdperken van de man*, Amsterdam, 1967, p. 25.
53. *Ideen*, vol. II, p. 63.
54. *Ibid.*, p. 70.

But this is not all. We must take into account the possibility that the genesis of my self can only be explained by the fact that whole layers or strata of my former conscious life are "buried." If this is the case, how can I as a philosopher come to know that? We will have to answer in general, through the experiences of other people, who were *other Egos for me* and who were older than I.

Later we will return to this point. For the present let us draw two conclusions from our analyses, one negative and the other positive. From the negative standpoint, we must declare that Husserl entertained too high expectations with respect to the range and import of reflection. He assumed that consciousness is perfectly transparent to one's own reflective observation: "All experiences ... are in principle open to perception," he tells us.[55] He postulated, moreover, that everything which has ever existed in my consciousness remains always there although it is later given in a different way.[56]

On the positive side, we must say that all forms of life known to us show upbuilding and demolition, assimilation and dissimilation, integration and disintegration and that, as we have said, development is unthinkable without profound changes —changes that imply modifications of structures. A dialectic philosopher will not hesitate to affirm this. But why does the phenomenologist hesitate to follow him in this?

6. Summary and Conclusions

Summary

Let us now summarize what we have learned from our critical analyses. We saw that the tendencies which have been decisive for phenomenological philosophizing can be grouped together under four different headings. At the same time, we realized that these tendencies are partly at cross purposes, instead of merely complementing one another. For this reason phenomenology — and in particular Husserl's classical phenomenology — in spite of its brilliant character, leaves a number of questions unanswered. We may list here the inner tensions which we have discovered in phenomenology.

First, phenomenology presents itself as a philosophy of intuition. But, on the other hand, it is a philosophy that relativizes and brackets what is given through intuition.

Secondly, the dialectic of reductions corresponds to a series of

---

55. "Alle Erlebnisse ... sind principiell wahrnehmungsbereit." *Ideen,* vol. I,
56. Cf., e.g., *Zur Phänomenologie des inneren Zeitbewusztseins,* pp. 68, 119; *Passive Synthesis,* Beilage VIII, pp. 365-382.

epistemological postulates. These postulates, however, do not flow from that which is described concretely.

Thirdly, intentionality is characterized as being-directed-to and as "aiming at." On the other hand, consciousness is described as a closed immanence, a monadic interiority.

Fourthly, as a genetic philosophy, phenomenology desires to describe the coming-to-be of consciousness and of the world of consciousness. On the other hand, it clings to the postulate of the indestructibility of all contents of consciousness and to the *a priori* character of the structures of consciousness.

Conclusions

These are the results of the examination of conscience which we have performed as phenomenological philosophers. We have to admit that we are faced with a fourfold quandary which is the source of numerous difficulties, uncertainties and seeming contradictions. And we feel obliged to ask ourselves: What should be done? Is the difficulty we have described insurmountable? Is it possible to get out of the quandary, not through compromise, nor by a pseudo-solution, but in a philosophically satisfactory way? Can phenomenological philosophy remain phenomenological; in other words, can the principal concerns of Husserl and other great phenomenologists remain the driving forces of its questioning, its search and reflection, without running the risk of becoming stranded upon the above-mentioned contradictions?

The answer is that it can be done, but only at the cost of radical changes. If we wish to avoid a sterile "scholasticism" in the sense we have attached to this term, we shall have to renounce two deeply ingrained prejudices. We shall have to realize that phenomenology cannot begin with an ego-logy; and secondly, that reflection cannot be its principal method. In other words, phenomenology will have to give up its monologal style of thought.

There are two grave reasons which demand this revision of phenomenological thinking. The first is that a philosophy which begins as an ego-logy will inevitably end with solipsism. This we intend to show in the subsequent chapters. The second and most obvious reason is the fact that starting with an Ego which reflects upon itself in total solitariness is in conflict with phenomenological data. For, if in accordance with the methodical demands of Husserl we simply describe what takes place, each one of us must admit that as soon as I become conscious I discover the other Ego who is older than I. Even when I, following the example of Descartes, lock myself in my room to busy myself with solitary philosophizing, I find other philosophers who have come before me and have engaged in philosophical reflec-

tion. Even if I am all alone when I engage in philosophical meditation, this reflection is, nevertheless, first of all a dialogue — perhaps
a critical dialogue — with other thinkers who have made me become
philosophically alive. This fact has, of course, a wider implication.
Looking backwards I realize that I came to conscious life only through
the consciousness of other people.

Once this is recognized and accepted as an essential structure of my
existence and as a necessity of being, the difficulties we have mentioned above are no longer insuperable.

Let us begin with the idea of intentionality. The statement that my
consciousness is intentional does not mean that it can constitute the
other as other — whatever such an expression might mean — but that
my consciousness necessarily maintains a relation to the other. This is
a necessary relationship because any finite consciousness is dependent
upon other conscious beings.

This also sheds some light on the question of intuition. That which
is first perceived now is not a spatially extended thing, a utensil or
"pure nature," but what is first perceived is the other. This we can
learn even from the implicit wisdom of phenomenological language
itself. "Bodily given" can only be someone who has a body; a "believing" relationship refers primarily to a "you"; and "personal presence"
obviously refers to the presence of a self, everything else being less
directly present to me. What a utensil or a thing is or what nature is,
I learn precisely through the intermediary of others. This point has a
bearing also on the life of perception. "Consciousness of fulfillment"
is obtained only from that which *we* behold; what I alone see and no
one else is a "phantom thing" but not a thing.[57] Hence the intuitive
character of human consciousness is intimately connected with its
social character.

But this is not all. By the fact that the other associates with me,
deals with me, speaks with me, I undergo a change. I am no longer
passive, helpless, speechless. As a partner, a fellow-worker with the
other, as one who contributes his own word, I am no longer the same
as I was. And if I change, there is then also a change in the world
around me. Even the other is no longer the same for me. The dialogue between the other and me enters into a new phase. Thus there
arises a dialectic that has characteristic phases; and these phases demand a careful description.

Now, how does the dialectic described above differ from the execu-
tion of the various reductions? The answer to that question is evident. This dialectic, this interplay between myself and the others,

---

57. Cf. *"Dingvorlesung."*

between me and my world-around-me, is no longer put into motion
by me as a sovereign and solitary consciousness. On the contrary, it is
first passively undergone by me, and then only, in response to what
has affected me, I actively take part in its completion. First I am being handled, then in turn I can handle; first I am loved and then in
turn I can love; first I am spoken to and then I can speak. The *cogitor*
(I am thought) comes before the *cogito* because, once more, the
"you" is older than the "I."

Thus we see that the dialectic which flows from this most original,
most general and necessary ontological situation is not an epistemological thought experiment. It is not an arbitrary change of attitude,
not an act which I can, at will, accomplish or not accomplish. It has
its roots in the things which I had to experience, perceive and undergo in order to become the one who at present I am. The dialogal dialectic, then, arises where freedom and necessity coincide for me; it
is a philosophical reflection upon my destiny.

Finally a word about the idea of genesis. This problem, too, must
be considered in the light of what we have explained above. If it is
true that my consciousness is originally awakened by another consciousness, then we must say that the life of consciousness is finite,
changeable and perishable. Then the *cogito* is not self-sufficient but
needy. If this is accepted, there is room for a genuinely genetic view.
Then there can be question of building up and tearing down, of the
formation and the disintegration of structures, of blooming and dying.
Then the genesis of my conscious life can obviously not be described
without taking into consideration that it is interwoven with other
conscious lives. Then, indeed, this genesis is merely one side of the
above-described dialogal dialectic.

The Task of Dialogal Phenomenology

These ideas, rapidly sketched above, call up a new series of questions. Some of the themes which we have mentioned in passing will
be considered in the following lectures. There is one doubt, however,
that demands a word of explanation here. Precisely people who are
familiar with phenomenological philosophy will be inclined to ask:
If the starting point of philosophizing is no longer the immanence of
my Ego, if the conscious life of this Ego is not an absolute, if the
method is no longer — at least, no longer in the first place — reflection upon one's own experience, then, by what right is this philosophy
called phenomenology?

The answer has already been prepared to some extent in the preceding considerations. It is true that a dialogal phenomenology will

in many respects differ from "classical" phenomenology. Its principal theme, however, is preserved almost intact. It is the same that
Eugen Fink formulated in 1933 with Husserl's approval.[58] The essential question of phenomenology is and remains that of the origin of
the world.[59]

The task of a dialogal phenomenology will be to describe how a
world arises for us in the dialogue between me and the other. It will
also examine the turning points of this dialogue and the corresponding changes of worlds. It will not neglect the drama of human existence. Dialogal phenomenology can fulfill this task because it accepts
the other as the most original datum of experience and draws from it
the most important conclusion: it presents itself as a philosophy of
finiteness.

---

58. "Die phänomenologische Philosophie Edmund Husserls in der gegenwär-
tigen Kritik," *Kantstudien*, vol. 38 (1933), pp. 329-383.
59. Concerning the concept of the world, see the following lecture.

LECTURE TWO

THE CONCEPT "WORLD" IN THE
PHILOSOPHY OF HUSSERL

1. Introductory Remarks: The Problem

The preceding chapter ended by saying that "dialogal phenomenology accepts the other as the most original datum of experience." The obvious thing is to proceed at once to an analysis of that unique experience, to describe it and arrange everything else around that central datum. But, from a philosophical standpoint, to do the obvious thing can be to choose the easy way. In our case, if we were to proceed that way, we would overlook two difficulties. One of these would be concerned with the content of our analysis, the other is a methodic difficulty.

With respect to the content, it is important to note that the other, even if we do not look upon him as the other Ego, is the other with respect to *me*. And who am I? Modern philosophers have not ceased to ask themselves that question since Descartes wrote his famous MEDITATIONS. Husserl's answer is: I am "an all-finding subject, even the subject for all objects, for the whole world";[1] Merleau-Ponty declares that "I am only a center of worldly situations";[2] and Sartre considers man's relation to the world as the concrete starting point of his philosophizing.[3] It is possible, then, that the phenomenologist's answer to the question, Who am I?, includes a reference to the world. But that answer remains meaningless if we do not know what is meant by the "world."

The methodic difficulty is connected with all this. Whoever has some philosophical experience knows that much — if not everything — depends on the way a question is formulated. Thus, in the present context, the concept "world" could play a decisive role from a negative or a positive standpoint. For example, must we, with Löwith, start from the concepts "world" and "surrounding world" (*Umwelt*) and from these concepts draw conclusions about the role of the other as my fellowman?[4] Or is it true, as Bingswanger writes, that the loving togetherness of you and me occurs in a special world that is completely dif-

---

1. "... ein alles vorfindendes Subjekt, eben das Subjekt für alle Objekte, für das Weltall." *Erste Philosophie,* vol. II, p. 71.
2. *Phénoménologie de la perception,* p. 520.
3. *L'être et le Néant,* p. 38.
4. *Das Individuum in der Rolle des Mitmenschen,* Darmstadt, 2nd ed., 1962.

ferent from the world of the man who is occupied with many cares?[5]
Or is Husserl right when he maintains that my Ego and the other Ego
are parts of a transcendental community of monads, and that "the"
world constitutes itself in the transcendental life of that community?
And, finally, what is the meaning of our statement that "a world arises
for us in the dialogue between me and the other"?[6] Again, one needs to
find out what an author means when he uses the term "world."

One might be inclined to think that the phenomenological philosophers have carefully defined that idea, which is so central in their
thinking. But this is not the case. Rather, one gets the impression that
each prominent phenomenologists, be he Scheler, Sartre, Merleau-
Ponty or Heidegger, use the term "world" in somewhat different
senses. We will confine ourselves, however, to Husserl and his idea of
world.

2. Three Concepts of "World"

Husserl actually describes what must be understood by "world" in
several very different ways. It would be necessary to undertake a pains-
taking, systematic examination if we desired to record, arrange and
compare *all* the shades of meaning which Husserl has explicitly defined or implicitly presupposed. But we will limit ourselves to a comparison between three essentially different notions of "world."

a. The Totality of Beings for Us

In the first place, Husserl designates by the term "world" the totality of beings for me or for us. "Is not all being," he asks rhetorically,
"conceived concretely determined and determinable, essentially being
in a universe of being, a world?"[7] In keeping with this notion, Husserl
the logician looks upon the world as the whole of all the substrata of
judgments, and he calls it the "all-being" (*Allseiende*) and the "all-
something" (*All-etwas*).[8] The world, he assures us, is not only a "world
of things" (*Sachenwelt*), but also a "world of values" (*Wertewelt*), a
"world of goods" (*Güterwelt*), a "practical world" (*Praktische Welt*).[9]
And after completing the reduction, I should realize that the same
world that appears to me as a "collective whole" of "positive validi-

---

5. *Grundformen und Erkenntnis menschlichen Daseins,* Munich, 3rd ed.,
1962, p. 71.
6. Cf. above, p. 22.
7. "Ist alles Seiende, konkret sachhaltig bestimmt und estimmbar gedacht,
nicht wesensmäszig Seiendes in einem Seinsuniversum, in einer Welt?" *Formale
und transzendentale Logik,* p. 134.
8. *Erfahrung und Urteil,* p. 157.
9. *Ideen,* vol. I, p. 59.

ties"[10] is in reality a totality of intentional poles and of constituted objects.

This thought also fits in with the idea that the world is the universe of everything that, for me, in any way whatsoever, has acquired reality. The words "for me" are, of course, very important. The world of which Husserl speaks is never the "totality of things," the universe in the rationalistic sense. The world always has the meaning of a "world for me," "for us," "for a community of monads," and it never means the totality of beings existing in themselves. Thus the reference to one or more subjects is essential for the concept of the world.

b. Structured Reality

We encounter a second concept of the world when Husserl no longer looks upon the world as a summing-up of "all-something" but as a structured whole. To his negative declaration that "the world is not a heap of things" there corresponds a positive demand for the study of "the structure of the world itself as truly being."[12] And Husserl adds: "Whatever changes the convictions of individuals concerning beings may undergo — from true reality to vain semblance and the like — the ever existing world nevertheless remains in its universally valid form of structure.[13]

The concept of structure we have just mentioned also justifies the distinction which Husserl makes between "surrounding world" and "world," a distinction which Scheler bases on entirely different criteria.[14] That which is always pre-given, that "in which" we live, act, determine values, or strive, is, correctly expressed, our "surrounding world" and not "the world." The "surrounding world" corresponds to the realm of experiences of a concrete we, to a community-of-life which, in a historical and social respect, possesses a particular character, a community of which the members understand one another.[15] From this we must strictly distinguish "the absolutely objective world-structure that pervades all 'surrounding worlds' of life-communities (or separate groups of men) that are 'communized' and self-contained, a structure

10. *Erste Philosophie*, vol. II, p. 151.
11. Manuscript A VII 20, quoted by Alvin Diemer, *Edmund Husserl*, Meisenheim a.L., 1956, p. 195.
12. "die Struktur des als seiend geltender Welt selbst." *Erste Philosophie*, vol. II, p. 151.
13. "Wie auch im einzelnen die Seinsüberzeugungen wechseln — aus schlechthin geltender Wirklichkeit nichtiger Schein wird und dergleichen — doch immer seiende Welt in ihrer allgemeingültigen Strukturgestalt verharrt ... " *Ibid.*
14. Cf. *Die Stellung des Menschen in Kosmos*, Munich, 3rd ed., 1949, pp. 39-41; *Philosophische Weltanschauung*, Bern, 1954, Dalp Series, vol. 301, pp. 29-31.
15. *Phänom. Psychologie*, Beilage XXVII, pp. 496 ff.

that everyone can understand and must be able to understand in order that men can at all exist for one another."[16]

At first sight, the difference between this concept of the world and the one mentioned before does not seem to be very great. Where the first spoke of a totality, one could say, the second speaks of a structured totality. But this explanation appears insufficient, for it takes no account of the explicitly mentioned possibility that the convictions of the experiencing subject may change, so that a true reality can become a vain semblance. As is well-known, Husserl has examined that possibility and followed it to its ultimate consequences. Even the entire totality of experiences could disclose itself as a connected dream.[17] But if the reality of the objects can undergo such radical changes while the world as world, in spite of all revolutions, ought to maintain itself, then we are forced to conclude that the world of which we are now speaking must be essentially independent from the worldly objects which for me and for us at a given moment possess reality. That world is then no longer a world of things, values and goods; it is a structure and nothing but a structure. For Husserl considers it self-evident that the structure of experience can remain the same, in spite of all the changes in the experienced contents.

In this second sense Husserl speaks of the world as a "structure of identity that is valid for all men."[18] And in his IDEAS he tells us: "An empty mist of vague indeterminateness becomes peopled with intuitive possibilities or probabilities and only the 'form' of the world, precisely as 'world,' is predelineated."[19] Thus we must distinguish a formal concept of the world from the material one which we have mentioned in the first place. These two concepts are dialectically related, but the first is essentially different from the second.

c. Horizon of All Experiencing Intentions

Husserl also describes the world in a third, entirely different way. In numerous published and unpublished writings he shows that the "world" is the horizon of all experiencing intentions, in fact, that it is the horizon of all intentions in general. In the latter sense Husserl

---

16. "... die durch alle Umwelten aller vergemeinschafteten und in sich geschlossenen Lebensgemeinschaften (oder Sondermenschheiten) hindurch gehende absolut objektive Weltstruktur, die jedermann in unbedingter Allgemeinheit erfassen kann und erfassen musz können, damit überhaupt Menschen füreinander da sein können." *Ibid.*, pp. 498 f.

17. *Cart. Medit.*, p. 57.

18. *Phänom. Psychologie*, p. 496.

19. "... ein leerer Nebel der dunkeln Unbestimmtheit bevölkert sich mit anschaulichen Möglichkeiten oder Vermutlichkeiten und nur die 'Form' der Welt, eben als 'Welt' ist vorgezeichnet." *Ideen*, vol. I, p. 59.

asserts that there is "permanently a horizon of validity, a world considered as real, over and beyond the detail that is singled out as relatively determined."[20]

This concept of the "world" is considered by Husserl's prominent followers and interpreters as most characteristic of his way of philosophizing. For example, Eugen Fink tells us that "with the introduction of the phenomenological analysis ... the universal horizon 'world' collapses."[21] Ludwig Landgrebe clarifies the concept of his teacher by saying: "The 'world' is not an object among other objects, but that which encompasses all the objects of experience, the ground of every single experience."[22] And in his unpublished thesis Herman Leo Van Breda compares the "world" as conceived by Husserl to a "universal receptacle."[23]

Of course, Husserl's idea can also be expressed in other terms. For example, in the IDEAS the world is characterized as "the general thesis of the natural attitude";[24] this expression implies that *the* general thesis differs essentially from all individual theses, in the sense that the general thesis is the "ground" upon which the other theses rest and from which they arise.

We must now try to investigate the philosophical significance attached to the metaphorical expressions of the phenomenologists when they speak of "ground" and "horizon."

The World as "Ground"

The first metaphor is not difficult to interpret. The "ground" is that upon which everything rests but that does not itself need any support. In this sense it could be said that belief in a world is that from which all conceivable intentions arise and that the world is the ground upon which all intentional objects rest. This implies that everything which is intentionally known, aimed at or practically manipulated, is already beforehand apperceived as "something in the world." Similarly, everything by which we are affected or stimulated stands out against the

---

20. " ... ständig ein Geltungshorizont, eine Welt in Seinsgeltung [ist], über das jeweils in Einzelheit und relativer Bestimmtheit Ergriffene . . . hinaus." *Erfahrung und Urteil,* p. 30.

21. "Mit dem Ingangbringen der phänomenologischen Analyse ... fällt der Universalhorizont 'Welt'." *Studien zur Phänomenologie, 1930-1939,* The Hague, 1966, p. 9.

22. "Welt ist kein Gegenstand unter anderen Gegenständen, sondern das alle Gegenstände der Erfahrung Umschlieszende, der Boden jeder Einzelerfahrung." *Der Weg der Phänomenologie,* Gütersloh, 1963, p. 54.

23. *De Transcendentaal Phaenomenologische Reductie in Husserls laatste periode (1920-1938),* manuscript, Louvain, 1941, P. II/12.

24. *Ideen,* vol. I, p. 63.

background of the world as something that affects or stimulates us. That is the reason why belief in an existing world is the universal ground of all activities and passivities.[25] But we should not lose sight of the fact that the ground of the world is unique as "ground." Being that which supports everything, it is the absolutely ultimate foundation; this cannot be said of any other ground.

Husserl, however, does not develop this thought in connection with the notion of "ground." To express it, he uses another figure and speaks of "horizon," a concept which he develops in numerous texts, clarifying and applying it.

The Concept "Horizon"

Let us consider here an experiencing intention. It culminates in a kind of knowledge which satisfies us. In Husserl's terminology, this means that the matter to be explored is finally present to me in the mode of being "itself there." Presumably the subject who has had this experience will now take no further steps to continue his exploration. But he has in principle the possibility to ask new questions, to transcend what is given for the purpose of exploring new determinations of the same thing. A consequence of this is that around the core of actual data there are formed, as it were, concentric centers of possible new explorations which are known only as to their general style. For example, I see a piece of furniture fairly well, but I am unable to discern the particular patterns in the grain of the wood. I know that I must get closer to that object to see the pattern and that, if I wish to see the other side, I must go around that piece of furniture and look again. The term "must" each time indicates a step forward beyond the actual experience. It is this kind of "concentric circles" of possible anticipating intentions related to the same object that Husserl calls an "inner horizon."[26]

Another essential possibility is that we can transcend the object that was first intended and aim at other objects. In a visual perception we see a particular object, but the room in which it is located appears only as a vague background. Nothing, however, prevents us from exploring that room itself in a subsequent act. At the same time, we are vaguely aware of the fact that the particular room is in a house, but the house itself and the location of the room in it are not objects of our present awareness. Neither do we really intend to study a blueprint of the house so as to determine the exact location of the room. We are attending to this only in the form of indefinite anticipations; and yet, wheth-

---

25. Cf. *Erfahrung und Urteil,* pp. 23-26.
26. Cf. *ibid.,* p. 28.

er we want it or not, we always make such anticipations. The vague possibilities that thus present themselves to our minds also form concentric circles around a given object. Husserl speaks of all this as an "external horizon."

Time consciousness, with respect to both the past and the future, also gives rise to the formation of a horizon.[27] I think, for example, that I know what will happen to me one hour from now, tomorrow or the next day, but with respect to what I can expect one year from now I have only a vague conjecture.

Husserl, moreover, speaks of a historical horizon,[28] an axiological and a practical horizon. (Where Heidegger develops his concept of the world and in connection with it has recourse to pragmatic references to "patterns of utensils" (*Bewandtnisganzheiten*), he develops Husserl's thought and gives it a new form.[29]) For us here, however, it is not necessary to give a complete enumeration of all imaginable worldly horizons. What is important is the question what all those horizons have in common and, respectively, what essential features are revealed by all forms of consciousness-of-horizon.

It is easy to answer this question on the basis of numerous Husserlian texts. One can say that a horizon arises whenever consciousness transcends the actual data in a particular meaningful way. For ininstance, consciousness is an insight into the fact that to S must be attributed predicates p and q, but there is, at the same time, a suspicion that other predicates possibly also belong to S; consciousness is the consciousness of a present time and an anticipation of a future; it is the consciousness of a "here" and a vague consciousness of a "there"; it is the consciousness of a limited series but also the consciousness of the possibility of "endlessly" extending the series by way of "and so on."[30] Husserl often speaks of "open horizons." This openness means that the horizon invites us ever anew to transcend that which has actually been grasped. All those descriptions agree; they give the impression of being unambiguous and clear.

3. *The Horizon and the World*

Absolute Horizon

Precisely for that reason one cannot help noticing that Husserl does not express himself in such a simple and clear way when he deals with the horizon of the world. He speaks, for instance, of "a vaguely con-

---

27. Cf. *Ideen,* vol. I, p. 58.
28. *Die Krise . . . ,* p. 324.
29. Cf. *Sein und Zeit,* p. 83.
30. Cf. *Erfahrung und Urteil,* p. 257.

scious horizon of an indefinite reality."[31] "a concentric circle of indefinite definiteness,"[32] "an empty horizon of unclearness and indistinc-
tiveness,"[33] "a structure of the known and unknown."[34] In an important fragment in which he tries to characterize the nature of flowing
transcendental life, Husserl tells us that this life "has its own living
but fluidly changing range — without strict limits and yet limited,
and limited in a varying fashion."[35]

Reading those texts, one is struck by the numerous contradictions
appearing in pairs, such as "limited-unlimited," "undetermined-deter-
mined," "unknown-known." There is, of course, no question of mere
"logical inconsistency." Husserl makes use of such apparent contradictions in order to describe that which defies every description, viz., the
horizon of the world.

This alone suffices to show that the horizon of the world cannot
simply be compared to worldly horizons. For it is the "total horizon,"
the "universal horizon," the "absolute horizon." "In it," that is in the
world, Husserl tells us, "everything is, but the world itself is not a
being-in-something."[36] What does he mean by these technical expressions? In all the above-described worldly horizons something determined stood out against something that was relatively undetermined;
for example, something that was intended against something that was
vaguely co-intended, or something that was actual against something
that was possible. Moreover, there were differences between the intentions and the forms of horizon-consciousness corresponding to those
intentions. For example, it was easy to distinguish a temporal horizon
from a spatial one.

"The horizon of the world," however, overarches all those opposi-
tions, and it does this in a twofold respect. On the one hand, the horizon of the world permits no further formation of a horizon. For the totality of beings can no longer contain a reference to a being that is
co-intended. On the other hand, this horizon is an ultimate fact. It is
impossible to transcend it by projecting further possibilities. What has

---

31. "...dunkel bewuszten Horizont unbestimmter Wirklichkeit..." *Ideen,*
vol. I. p. 58.
32. "...Hof unbestimmter Bestimmtheiten..." *Ibid.,* p. 160.
33. "Leerhorizont der Unklarheit und Undeutlichkeit..." *Erste Philosophie,*
vol. II, p. 163.
34. "...Struktur der Bekanntheit und unbekanntheit..." *Erfahrung und
Urteil,* p. 33.
35. "...seine lebendige, aber strömend sich ändernde Reichweite hat — ohne
eigentliche Grenze und doch begrenzt, und veränderlich begrenzt." *Erste Philosophie,* vol. II, Beilage XXVII, p. 467.
36. "In ihr [in der Welt] ist alles, sie selbst aber ist nicht ein Inetwas."
Erfahrung un Urteil, p. 157.

been said previously with respect to "ground" can be applied here in an analogous way. All comparisons of, and all relations to worldly beings presuppose the horizon of the world; on that account the world itself is beyond comparison. It is the horizon of all horizons. In this sense it is the absolute horizon.

Horizon and Limit

Must we, then, conceive the horizon of the world as an absolute limit? As long as we cling to the image of the horizon, we will be inclined to answer in the affirmative, for we are then thinking in terms of our perceptual experience. When, for example, we look at a landscape, we see clearly that which is close to us; what is far away we see only vaguely, and finally we no longer see anything. The wealth of visual data keeps decreasing until there is an absolute emptiness. The horizon, so it seems, "limits" the field of vision. Of course, the limit is changeable; our field of vision widens, for instance, when we climb a tower or a mountain. But, no matter how much effort we make to enlarge our field of vision, it is and remains limited. The limit retreats but it continues to exist. The horizon, we would say in everyday life, is a "line" that "limits" our field of vision. And yet, even in everyday life, if we were asked where that line is, we would not know what to say. But is a line that, in principle, cannot be localized conceivable at all?

Thus one can understand why Husserl had recourse to the contradictory formula "without strict limits and yet limited." Why is a horizon not a strict limit? The answer to that is unambiguous. A horizon is not a limit because a limit or boundary is "drawn," it is the result of a determination, of an act of "setting" a real or ideal determination. The limits or boundaries of a piece of land, for example, are fixed within the framework of the intersubjective economic activities of men. Similarly, the limits or boundaries of a country depend on the political vicissitudes of its inhabitants and the neighboring peoples. The two examples have this in common that, when the boundary line is being drawn, that which lies on the other side of the boundary is at least implicitly taken into account. The owner knows that someone else's property begins on the other side of the stone marking the boundary; the inhabitants of a country know that on the other side of a particular line there are people who belong to a different nation. In short, the concept of boundary or limit can serve as an exemplar for dialectical thinking. By positing the boundary or limit, consciousness, at the same time, removes it.[37]

---

37. Cf. Hegel, *Wissenschaft der Logik*, ed. by G. Lasson, Leipzig, 2nd ed., 1932, vol. I, pp. 110 ff.; *System der Philosophie*, Jubiläumausgabe, Stuttgart, 1963, vol. VIII, pp. 245 ff.

Thinking Also Is Thinking in the World

Something analogous can be said with respect to other forms of hori-
zonal consciousness. Abstract thinking is no exception in that regard.
Let us choose a series of numbers, an algebraic or geometric series, to
serve as an example. Husserl calls such mental creations "constructive
infinities." They owe their origin to iterative thought achievements.
Such an iteration is actually finite, but the thinker dissembles his
finiteness through the above-mentioned expressions "and so forth" and
"we can always once more." Husserl adds here the important observation that this "we can always once more" is "a manifest idealization,
for *de facto* no one 'can always once more'."[38] This shows that the "constructive infinities" of the human mind are actually finite. They issue
into the void of something that could ideally be thought but is not
really thought.

To this we may add our reflection concerning the possibility of comparing worldly horizons. It is not difficult to establish that, for example, an ensemble of theoretical references differs from a pragmatic
whole of references. But generally we do not ask ourselves on what
ground we make such judgments. Within what horizon can we make
a comparison between real beings and ideal beings? What enables us
to connect and relate totally different relative infinities to one another?

These considerations prevent us from characterizing the universal
horizon as a "form." A form is essentially different from something
that is relatively unformed or formless. A form is in contrast with a
backgrond, with something indefinite, something devoid of order,
a chaos. A form, moreover, is not essentially different from other
forms. The horizon of the world, on the contrary, is unique. One
could also say that a form is a being of thought. The horizon of the
world permits us, precisely, to think of, compare and determine beings, to discover relationships between them and to proceed to make
abstractions. The "world," conceived as a universal horizon, evidently
is not a being, nor the totality of beings, nor a structure of beings.

It is only this third concept of the world — and no other — that
enables us to pass on to an interpretation of certain phenomena that
fascinated Husserl. We are thinking, for example, of the peculiar fact
that "all individual objects of experience are pre-known."[39] This phenomenon could, in the last analysis, be interpreted as follows: the

---

38. "Es [das 'Man kann immer wieder'] ist eine offenbare Idealisierung, da
de facto niemand immer wieder kann." *Formale und transzendentale Logik*, p.
176.

39. ". . . Vorbekanntheit jedes einzelnen Gegenstandes der Erfahrung." *Erfahrung und Urteil*, p. 26.

world as universal horizon ties together into a unity all the beings which are objects of actual and possible experience. That is why we feel at home in the world and why we are able to "dwell" in it. Our familiarity with worldly beings is so great that certain divergent experiences do not shake our confidence. Such experiences make us face a "problem"; in this respect they can be compared to a blank spot on a map. We do not know exactly what beings are found in that place, but we can imagine their general character and we have also certain conjectures as to how we should be able to know them. This may help to explain why "problems" do not detract from our anticipatory knowledge of worldly beings and from the style of those experiences by which they are fundamentally capable of being known and grasped by us.[40]

Experience also is the foundation for the coherence of the syntactic matter of a judgment. This is important for the solution of a problem which most logicians did not even see — namely, the possibility of making a judgment. For instance, why may we not say that this table is true and that judgment is brown? Husserl demonstrates that every original judgment owes its coherence to the synthetic unity of the experience which is its foundation. Now, as we have seen, the universal foundation of all experience is the world.[41]

Going somewhat farther in the spirit of Husserl, could we not ask ourselves whether the absolute unity of the world is not the mysterious original image and exemplar to which our thought owes its power to form logical wholes that are not self-contradictory, whether the perfect self-identity of the world is not the hidden guideline that enables us to posit identifying acts? The elementary formal rules of logic — the inborn principles of reason — would then have a worldly ground, with this restriction, however, that, according to Husserl's mind, this ground, in its turn, must be clarified in a transcendental philosophical way.

The Many Meanings of the Term "World"

We have seen that Husserl makes use of at least three concepts of the "world" that are essentially different from one another. To characterize and situate them better, it may be useful to compare them with other meanings that the term "world" can have in the language of philosophy and science as well as in everyday usage.[42]

1. The world as *cosmos* means the orderly whole made up of the earth together with the heavenly bodies; in other words, the universe.

---

40. *Formale und Transzendentale Logik,* p. 208.
41. *Ibid.,* p. 194.
42. The following sketch is only meant as an orientation; it does not claim to be complete.

2. As *orbis terrarum* the world is the sublunary reality comprising the earth with its five continents.

3. In the technical language of philosophy it is customary to use the term "world" in reference to the independently existing totality of all finite actual beings. Alexander Baumgarten, for example, defines the "world" (*mundus*) as "the series (multitude, whole) of the actual finite beings, which is not a part of another series."[43] In this sense the "world" is virtually the same as the "universe."

4. It is also possible to place the emphasis on the way the finite beings are united into a whole. This is done, for instance, by Leibniz. He sees the "world" as that, among all complete and "co-possible" systems, which God in His wisdom has actually realized.[44]

5. A special place belongs to Kant's concept of the "world." In his "antinomies" Kant proves that a consistent consideration of the synthetic whole of the world leads to insoluble contradictions.[45] He looks upon the "world" as a regulative idea that makes knowledge possible according to the principles of a totality.[46] The accent, then, is placed upon the formal element of knowledge. On the other hand, we should not forget that Kant was the first philosopher to connect the notion of the "world" with the knowing, experiencing and thinking subject.

6. In common parlance, as well as in technical scientific and philosophical usage, one can say that the term "world" refers to a multitude composed of finite entities constituting a relatively closed whole and obeying typical laws. Not only are physical systems called by that name (for instance, the world of atoms or micro-organisms), but also metaphysical regions (the "sensible world" and the "intelligent world"), typical fields of experience (the "inner world" and the "outer world"), and realms of thought (the "world of numbers"). In this sense it is possible, therefore, to speak of a multitude of worlds, of many worlds.

7. A sector of reality that is experienced by a particular kind of subject in a typical way can be called a "world" in prescientific as well as scientific language. For example, Jacob von Uexküll speaks of the "perceived world" (*Merkwelt*) and the "world of action" (*Wirkwelt*) of living beings; and one can refer to the "world of the child" or the "world of primitive man."

8. In a theistic philosophy or a monotheistic theology the world is the totality of created reality. This reality bears witness to the existence of God, but is not itself divine.

---

43. *Metaphysica,* par. 354.
44. *Theodicee,* vol. 2, par. 414-416.
45. *Kritik der reinen Vernunft,* bk. 2, ch. 2.
46. *Prolegomena . . . ,* par. 56.

9. Christian theology teaches that created reality can, and even is inclined to, turn against its Creator. From that standpoint the terms "world," "worldly" and "mundane" acquire a pejorative meaning. The *cosmos*, as Karl Löwith observes,[47] changes into the *saeculum*, the sinful world that is estranged from God, proud and autarkic.

When we now compare the three different concepts of the world that are used by Husserl with this list, we see that his first two are not original. The "material" concept of the world is somewhat connected with the seventh meaning listed above. But we must abstract here from the typical meaning which the words "particular subjects" in that concept acquire after the completion of the transcendental-phenomenological reduction.

In connection with Husserl's concept of "world-form" or "world-structure" one could perhaps think of Leibniz. For Husserl repeatedly speaks of the problem of "co-possible worlds" and when he does he explicitly refers to Leibniz.[48] Sometimes he also calls the world an *a priori*, thereby calling up Kantian and neo-Kantian memories.[49]

The only Husserlian concept of the world which is original is the third one. It does not agree with any of the meanings we have enumerated above in our survey. Moreover, it cuts across the usual divisions. For instance, when the metaphysician visualizes the Platonic world of ideas or when the Christian theologian speaks of angelic choirs, these are, phenomenologically speaking, worldly representations. This phenomenological position, however, has nothing to do with either Christian or post-Christian views. According to the phenomenological way of considering things, all sectors of beings, all ontological regions, are surrounded by one and the same all-encompassing horizon; the latter embraces the sublunary as well as the *topos ouranios*, the material cosmos as well as immaterial realities.

4. One World and Many Worlds

Interconnection of the Three Concepts of "World"

Leaving aside for the time being the interpretation of Husserl, let us ask ourselves how his three concepts of the world are mutually related and interconnected. This question can be asked apart from all philosophical considerations, for even in daily parlance we speak of "the" world and, at the same time, say that "everyone has his own little world." How is it that we blissfully accept such a clear-cut contradiction?

---

47. *Der Weltbegriff in der neuzeitlichen Philosophie,* Heidelberg, 1960, p. 22.
48. Cf., e.g., *Cart. Medit.,* p. 167.
49. Cf., e.g., *ibid.,* p. 165.

One thing we have already ascertained, viz., there is a connection between the material and the formal concept of "world." But the foundation on which that connection rests is not yet clear. Perhaps it is possible to clarify that connection by means of the concept of "horizon." A horizon, we saw, is called up whenever consciousness transcends actual data in a particular meaningful way. If we now pass on from the horizon to that which is enclosed by it, we can say that the above-mentioned actual data, together with further data suspected, anticipated or considered possible thanks to my transcendent act, in a material sense form a world of consciousness.

Here it is not required that the data spoken of should have a reference to observable, spatially extended or concrete beings. For we rightly speak, for instance, of a "world of numbers." This world exists for us by the fact that we actually think of some numbers and, at the same time, co-intend an infinite series of numbers as an ideal possibility of thought. The actually grasped quantites and those that are anticipated then form together a relatively closed whole which obeys typical laws. This agrees with the sixth sense of the term "world" mentioned in our survey.[50]

Moreover, in our description of "horizon" there was question of a "particular meaningful way" in which the actual data are transcended. The manner of transcending is evidently different when it is a question of a spatial or a temporal horizon, or of the pragmatic horizon of the man who is occupied with caring for things. But there is one thing that all acts which transcend in a meaningful way have in common — namely, they call to life a particular order, a particular structure. For human consciousness grasps the data immediately, and not only through an act of reflection, in the light of a particular way of giving meaning. For example, these data are things that are found together in a particular space; events that follow one another; or tools that refer to one another. Hence a world without order, without structure, is unthinkable. That is why we must introduce the formal concept of the world beside the material one.

The manner in which the meaningful order is projected can also vary. As we saw, this manner is typical for particular individuals or groups. And it is not difficult to show that this is so. For the educated Western man the meaningful order of the world rests on causal connections, but for a small child it is magical. This means that for the mature man there exist X-rays and microbes; but for the child there is Santa Claus and Father Christmas. In other words, the "world-material" is not independent of the "world-form." At the same time,

---

50. Cf. above, p. 34.

our examples show that such "worlds" are not accidentally but necessarily many. For the "style" of the transcending process, the nature of
the projected principle of order, is connected with the mode of existing of those for whom this or that world is a world; and these existences are, on their part, not wholly independent from bodily, social
and historical conditions.

From all this we can draw a twofold conclusion:

1. The formal and the material concepts of the world are indissolu-
bly connected.

2. The formally and materially determined world appears as many
because of the diversity of possible determinations. To avoid misunderstandings therefore we will hereafter speak of "worlds."

Relationship of the Many Worlds to the One World for All

The big question that now calls for our attention can be exactly
formulated in this way: how do the worlds that differ from the formal
and the material standpoint relate to the one world that is the world
for all?

Let us begin by eliminating all pseudo-solutions. One can readily
assume that *the* world is made up of a multitude of worlds, but from
what has been said above it is clear that that is a false representation.
For "worlds" refers to wholes or totalities of beings, as they appear to
human subjects; *the* world, on the contrary, refers to the universal
horizon that embraces all beings, including also all subjects — all men
and groups of men — for whom there exist worlds in the plural. It is
evident, therefore, that it is not in the direction of the relationship of
whole and part that we must look for a solution.

Similarly, it is not very meaningful to declare that *the* world is
something objective whereas the world*s* are different subjective modes
in which that one objective datum appears. This is evident from the
very fact that, although the world*s* can be regarded as totalities of
beings which appear to particular individuals and groups of men,
the world can in no way be called a totality of beings. Hence there is
no question here of one and the same entity that is known now in an
objective and then in a subjective way. On the contrary, the more we
think about it, the more the essence of *the* world is seen to differ completely from the essence of the many world*s*.

The solution of our problem, then, must be sought on another level,
namely, that of ontological thought. As we have repeatedly noted,
worlds are relatively closed totalities of beings-for-us that exhibit a
particular structure. But is a horizon a being? And, especially, is the
universal horizon, which envelops us together with all beings-for-us, a
being? De Waelhens does not hesitate to give a negative answer to

that question. On the other hand, he insists that the world necessarily stands in a definite relationship to what is. And, in connection with this, he points to the phenomenon from which we have started. It is certain that we could not speak of a horizon if there existed no landscape. In an analogous way we must say that if there were no beings, neither would there be the universal horizon of the world. *The* world is the bond that makes beings be for one another. But this does not yet mean that *the* world may be regarded without any more ado as a being.[51]

Perhaps we must go even further. De Waelhens is right when he insists that the world is not "nothing"; for otherwise it could not stand in a relationship to what is. The world is indeed not "nothing," but it is a "no" with respect to what is. By its "no" it testifies that it is not a being. So the big question is, where, then, does this "no" come from?

Let us start with De Waelhens' thesis that the horizon of the world is the bond that makes beings be for one another. It is then also that which makes the beings be present to me in the form of a structured totality. It ties them together and enables me to perceive, think, use and handle them, but only in a particular perspective, on the basis of a particular view. Why is that so? Why am I unable to avoid that hampering perspective? Why must I make one meaningful view my own and not another? Why does the rationalistic dream of the universe of beings that the spirit can freely survey, judge and order not agree with reality? Is this perhaps connected with the fact that we are not the spirit but a multitude of finite, bodily-spiritual beings? Isn't this our actual situation? Doesn't this facticity make a decisive contribution? If this is the case, then the great "no" that the horizon of the world calls out to us is connected with our finiteness, our facticity, our non-transcendental way of existing. The world is then a shadow cast by our finiteness upon the being of beings.

Two consequences flow from this idea:

1. Because of our finiteness, we are all surrounded by the same universal horizon and, together with all finite beings, we are for and with one another. In this sense we all "dwell" and have our home in the same world, and the world is a world-for-us.

2. Because of our facticity — our being bodily, historically, socially in this way and not in that way — our endeavors to survey, think and structure that whole are made in different ways. We therefore "see" worldly beings in different ways from the material as well as the for-

---

51. *La philosophie et les expériences naturelles,* The Hague, 1961, pp. 119-121.

mal standpoint. Thus there is question of many worlds. These worlds are, of course, unthinkable without *the* world. An attempt to endow the whole of the beings-for-us in a theoretical and a practical respect with a meaning can only be undertaken when that whole-for-us exists. *The* world, therefore, is the conditon that makes the origin of world*s* possible.

The worlds-for-us owe their origin and existence to some extent to our giving of meaning. In this limited sense — which we will more fully explain later — one can say that we "constitute" those worlds. In this second sense also one can say that human consciousness dwells in the world, but the latter now has a different meaning. The statement means that every human consciousness, together with other human consciousnesses, considers one of the many worlds that are materially and formally determined as *his* world. These worlds can rightly be compared to "homes," that is, like a home, they arise through an active-receptive interplay of conscious beings and, in this sense they are "constituted." *The* world, on the contrary, precedes all our choosing, projecting and meaning-giving activities. This has not always been correctly understood by the existential phenomenologists.

Transcendental phenomenology, on the other hand, is primarily concerned with *the* world. This is the great theme of its inquiries; and the main method that must be used for this purpose is the transcendental-phenomenological reduction.

5. The Problem of the Reduction of the World

The Transcendental-phenomenological Reduction

For the transcendental phenomenologist everything we have said thus far about the all-embracing and unique character of the world is but an introduction to the formulation of his principal thesis. This thesis reads as follows: *the* world with its worldly beings, its regions of being and structures, does not owe its validity as a really existing world to me, this individual man, but to the transcendental subjectivity that is active in me also. Of this I am not conscious while I am involved in the world by knowing, evaluating, manipulating, or striving for things. But when I suspend my belief in the reality of the world and that of worldly beings, then those beings change into phenomena for me. I then realize that they owe their reality and their meaning exclusively to me, to the extent that I share in the achieving life of transcendental subjectivity. I discover that life not only in myself but also in other monads with whom I am connected in a transcendental community of monads. Thanks to transcendental self-experience, I can scientifically describe the world-constituting life with its diverse intentional achievements, as well as the general and necessary structures that are determinative of those achievements. This scientific description is the chief task of transcendental phenomenology.

There are numerous obscurities in the doctrine of the transcendental-phenomenological reduction. The concepts "constitution," "achievement" and "transcendental communities of monads" are not sharply defined, and the same holds for the relationship between me, this individual man, and me, as this transcendental monad. Numerous philosophers have tried to interpret these concepts.[52] Moreover, the whole doctrine of transcendental-phenomenological reduction has met with much opposition; and the objections were numerous and persistent. The older Husserl repeatedly complained that only a few philosophers had followed him in his turn toward transcendental idealism.

We shall not deal with that question here but concentrate our attention on a single point. This point is, of course, not whether the world can be deprived of its reality. We already know that the "world" *is* not in the way a being *is*. In our opinion the decisive questions to be asked are the following two:

1. Is it possible to abolish the "world" as the universal horizon?

2. Is it possible to speak of a transcendental life that is a "worldless" life?

To answer these two questions, let us ask ourselves, in turn, What remains as a "residue" after the completion of the transcendental-phenomenological reduction? The realm of achieving life, what is it like? How actually does the constituting of *the* world operate? Husserl has given us several divergent descriptions of transcendental life, but two typical descriptions turn up repeatedly in his works.

---

52. Cf., e.g., Eugen Fink, *Studien zur Phänomenologie;* Ludwig Landgrebe, *Der Weg der Phänomenologie,* Gütersloh, 2nd ed., 1967; G. Berger, *Le cogito dans la philosophie de Husserl,* Paris, 1941; H. L. Van Breda, see footnote 23; M. Farber, *The Foundation of Phenomenology,* Cambridge, Mass., 1943; E. Levinas, *En découvrant l'existence avec Husserl et Heidegger,* Paris, 1947; A de Waelhens, *Phénoménologie et vérité,* Paris, 1953; A Gurwitsch, *Field of Consciousness,* Pittsburgh, 1964; R. Boehm, "Husserl et l'idéalisme classique," *Revue philosophique de Louvain,* vol. 57 (1959), pp. 351-396; Boehm, "Les ambiguïtés des concepts husserliens d' 'immanence' et de 'transcendance', *ibid.* vol. 59 (1959), pp. 481-526; I. Kern, *Husserl und Kant,* The Hague, 1964; A. Schutz, *Collected Papers,* 2 vols., The Hague, 1966; G. Funke, *Zur transzendentalen Phänomenologie,* Bonn, 1957; Funke, *Phänomenologie-Metaphysik oder Methode,* Bonn, 1966; Th. de Boer, *De ontwikkelingsgang in het denken van Husserl,* Assen, 1966.
53. *Zur Phänomenologie des inneren Zeitbewusztseins,* p. 83.

The first of these makes use of the ancient image of the stream. Husserl describes transcendental life as "the absolute stream of consciousness" in which the experiences form immanent temporal units. Consciousness as immanent unity is, at the same time, necessarily consciousness of objects in which it is intentionally involved.[54] The world then appears to be the ensemble of the objects that constitute themselves in the absolute stream of consciousness. I arrive at this understanding, of course, only after I have completed the transcendental-phenomenological reduction. As Husserl expresses it, "If, then, I complete the reduction with respect to everything, I acquire my transcendental subjectivity in its immanent temporal course of life and, enclosed in it, the universe of my actual or possible experiences and the thereto-related 'doxic' meanings and other acts, with their world-phenomenon."[55]

Elsewhere Husserl gives a different description of the reduction and the insight that results from it. The reduction consists there in a double split of the Ego. Insofar as I am a philosophical observer, "I" see myself as a human being who is interested in worldly reality; and I also understand that this man is only the *cogitatum* (the "thought-of") of a "cogitating" transcendental Ego. In his Paris lectures Husserl expressed himself as follows: "With the phenomenological reduction there comes about a sort of I-splitting. The transcendental observer places himself above himself; he looks at himself and also sees himself as the man who was formerly involved in the world; in other words, he finds himself in himself as *cogitatum* and he finds in the *cogitationes* of this man the whole world-constituting life."[56]

There is question here, then, of three different Egos: an Ego that merely observes; an Ego that, without knowing it, constitutes worldly beings which, together, form a world; and a third Ego that is the product of a "constituting" activity. Now, in order to be able to draw that "model," one must compare the functions of these three Egos, and these Egos must be looked upon as having a certain interconnection. But then the question arises at to the "ground" or basis used in com-

---

54. *Ibid.*, p. 96.
55. "Vollziehe ich dann an allem Reduktion, so gewinne ich meine transzendentale Subjektivität in ihrem immanent zeitlichen Lebensverlauf und darin beschlossen das Universum meiner wirklichen und möglichen Erfahrungen und der darauf bezogenen doxischen Meinungen und sonstigen Akte, mit ihrem Weltphänomen . . ." *Phänomenologische Psychologie,* Beilage XXI, p. 533.
56. "Mit der phänomenologischen Reduktion vollzieht sich eine Art Ich-Spaltung. Der transzendentale Zuschauer stellt sich über sich selbst, sieht sich zu und sieht auch als den vordem welthingegebenen Menschen, findet sich also in sich als cogitatum sich als Menschen und findet an den zugehörigen cogitationes das [das] gesamte weltliche ausmachende Leben." *Cart Medit.,* p. 16.

paring, distinguishing and connecting those Egos. Where does the philosopher "stand" while he is pursuing those thematic activities?

A second point is to be considered, viz., the fact that with the removal of the universal horizon of *the* world all other worldly horizons should also have been eliminated. Hence Husserl maintains that the transcendental Ego "no longer even has a horizon."[57] In other words, I, the transcendental onlooker, can survey my whole transcendental life without any perspective, any obscurity, any horizon. And yet, even after the reduction, he still speaks of an "endless horizon of remembrance and expectation,"[58] "degrees of clarity,"[59] a hidden Ego, [60] etc. How is this possible?

Our answer to this question is as simple as it is radical. We maintain that the transcendental phenomenologist, even after completing the transcendental reduction, can only describe worldly phenomena. In other words, what he describes is a world; although this world looks different from the world of any ordinary experience, it is a world all the same.

The model of the stream of consciousness is a good example to illustrate the point. For how do we know that absolute stream? Particular experiences of the stream of consciousness are directly given to us; others are anticipated through a transcendent expectation. Here, too, there is question of an infinity that "presumptively" belongs to it.[61] All immanent units of experience, moreover, are thought of as being ordered according to one principle of order, viz., the temporal flux of consciousness. All this is in agreement with the definition we have given of a world that is materially and formally determined.[62] With the proper changes, it agrees also with the connection between the three Egos, the observing, the constituting and the constituted Ego. They, too, appear in a worldly perspective. Certain acts of constituting, certain constituted objects corresponding to these acts, as well as certain observations of the disinterested onlooker that are related to them, are presented as given; others are anticipated as possibilities. The structural relationships between the three "instances" and their respective functions are also established. Why, then, shouldn't the spectacle presented by those three Egos with their activities and passivities be called a "world"?

Accordingly, what the transcendental phenomenologist describes as the origin of *the* world in fact refers only to *a* world. But this is

57. *Ibid.,* p. 107.
58. *Erste Philosophie,* vol. II, p. 86.
59. *Zur Phänomenologie des inneren Zeitbewusztseins,* p. 47.
60. *Erste Philosophie,* vol. II, p. 90.
61. *Cart. Medit.,* p. 55.
62. See above, pp. 36 f.

not all. In all descriptions, analyses and examinations of the transcendental phenomenologist there is always the tacit presupposition of the universal horizon. This horizon overarches the world as it presents itself in the "natural attitude"; it also overarches the ground of the world discovered — at least putatively — through the reduction. The relationship of that ground to that which it supports could not be conceived without the "bond" that makes something be for something else.[63] In short, the wish to get rid of the world's universal horizon would be equivalent to an attempt to ignore the finiteness of human consciousness. Such an attempt obviously does not lead anywhere.

It is not difficult to foresee what the transcendental phenomenologist will say in answer to our critique of the reduction. He will point out that the phenomenologist, in communicating with others, has only worldly concepts at his disposal and that he cannot help making use of the language of the "natural attitude." But we cannot attach much weight to this answer. A philosophy is an ensemble of expressed thoughts. It is essentially poetry, speech, dialogue, discussion, instruction, interpretation, meditation. The philosopher talks to himself or speaks with others. In both cases the horizon of the world is presupposed. Hence the idea of a philosophy that would be thought out without language, against language or beyond language must be rejected as self-contradictory.

Husserl's Hesitations

Our critique of the transcendental-phenomenological reduction may seem to be foolhardy. Fortunately we can appeal to a thinker whose authority in the field of phenomenology is admitted by all — viz., Husserl himself. The historical Husserl was, in fact, not as certain as is generally assumed about the possibility of doing away with the world. His hesitations find expression, among other things, when he asks the question whether the existence of the world can be called apodictically evident.

In the CARTESIAN MEDITATIONS a careful doubt is prudently formulated concerning the apodictic character of that evidence.[64] Husserl sometimes uses the term "relative apodicticity."[65] In unpublished writings he speaks of the "certainty of the world" as an "apodictic presumption." This, at first sight, looks like a contradiction in adjecto, for a "presumption" can never give a thing to us as "itself" given. We must, however, take into account that behind a seeming contradiction

---

63. See above, p. 38.
64. Cart Medit., p. 57.
65. Erste Philosophie, vol. II, Beilage XIII, p. 397.

a profound insight may be hidden. Husserl calls "apodictic" an evidence which "is not merely certainty of the affairs or affair-complexes evident in it; rather it discloses itself to a critical reflection as having the signal peculiarity of being at the same time the absolute unimaginableness of their non-being."[66] A critical reflection upon the horizon of the world once more presupposes that horizon. And it is this precisely that the preceding considerations have proved.

An important manuscript of Husserl that probably dates back to 1933 bears the title ABOUT THE APODICTIC PRESUMPTION OF THE WORLD. Husserl tells us there : "On the other hand, a doubt about the existence of the world is ridiculous. It is clear that the dignity of the experience of the world has a higher dignity of evidence than the one that belongs to the experience of an individual reality .... The existence of the world possesses a kind of apodicticity. It is not right that this is subject to doubt in me who experiences the world."[67]

In another manuscript he even says: "The world is and remains that which is valid for me — reduction does not change that fact."[68] We do not claim, it may be added, that the apodicticity of the world is a thesis that forms part of the official transcendental-phenomenological doctrine. But it is certain that Husserl did think along this line.

6. Conclusions

What consequences will follow for phenomenological thinking from the fact that the world is once more taken seriously? Will this fact change it into a superficial common-sense philosophy? Or will only now its original central ideas be able to exercise their full power? Everything depends on our firm determination inexorably to draw the necessary philosophical consequences from the apodicticity of the world. We would like to present here briefly four conclusions.

1. If the world is the universal horizon of all beings, then these beings are finite. This conclusion applies also to spiritual beings, conscious beings, intentionally involved beings. The problem how the Spirit "becomes finite"[69] then appears to be a pseudo-problem.

---

66. " ... nicht blosz Seinsgewiszheit der in ihr evidenten Sachen und Sachverhalte ist, sondern sich durch eine kritische Reflexion zugleich als schlechthinnige Unausdenkbarkeit des Nichtseins derselben enthüllt." *Cart. Medit.*, p. 56.

67. "Anderseits ist der Zweifel an dem Sein Welt lächerlich. Es ist klar, dasz die Dignität der Welterfahrung von einer höheren Dignität der Evidenz ist wie diejenige der Einzelerfahrung ... Die Weltexistenz hat etwas von Apodiktizität an sich; es ist nicht richtig, dasz dies für mich, da ich sie in Erfahrung habe, bezweifelbar ist." Stenographic manuscript B I 13/II; p. 13 in the transcript.

68. "Die Welt ist und bleibt die mir geltende — daran ändert die Reduktion nichts." Stenographic manuscript B I 5/IX, p. 27, quoted by Gerd Brand, *Welt, Ich und Zeit*, The Hague, 1955, p. 32.

69. Cf., e.g., Sartre, *L'être et le néant*, pp. 361-363.

In addition, concepts such as *the* consciousness, *the* mind and *the* transcendental life are then misleading and should be avoided. Phenomenology begins as a philosophy of finiteness. Finiteness cannot even be called the most descriptive characteristic; rather it is the condition which makes any real description possible.

2. If the horizon of the world is the condition on which intentional achievements can arise, then the intentional giving of meaning does not start exclusively from an autonomous consciousness. The consciousness of a finite being does not possess that kind of sovereignty. On the contrary, it must also be able to relate itself passively, receptively; it must also be able to receive meaning.

3. If the horizon of the world is *de facto* always something that is pre-given, then facticity and what is immediately connected with this, namely, the contingency and transitoriness of finite beings — including conscious beings — must once more be taken seriously. Expressed in a negative way, the recognition of the facticity of consciousness cannot be reconciled with the ruthless attempt to make this consciousness an absolute. It cannot be the task of phenomenological philosophy to describe the incomprehensible solitary play of a spirit. If descriptions are really the important thing, then it is finite man and his varying relationships to other finite men that must from the very beginning be at the focal point of philosophical interest. Only then will it be possible for the phenomenologist to delve deeply into the great problems of philosophical anthropology in a consistent manner and with a good philosophical conscience.

4. Among these great problems we find that of the active-receptive relationship of man and of human groups to their materially and formally determined worlds. The origin and disappearance of those worlds must be explained and described. But this will then no longer be a problem of transcendental philosophy but of a dialogal philosophy.

LECTURE THREE

FROM A PHENOMENOLOGY OF THE WORLD
TO A DIALOGAL PHENOMENOLOGY

1. A Pluralistic View of the World Problem

Unicity of the World; Plurality of Worlds

Our analysis of Husserl's concept of "world" had led to a positive result. It enabled us to ascertain that we are dealing with two different phenomena — namely, *the* world for all and, on the other hand, worlds that are worlds of a concrete "we" or a concrete "I." Now we must ask ourselves, How do those phenomena arise? With respect to the universal horizon, as we have already seen, this phenomenon is called forth by the fact that the transcending movement of corporeal-spiritual beings is finite and incomplete. This also explains why the horizon of *the* world is experienced as the same by all finite corporeal-spiritual beings.

What is more important, however, is that the "original situation," sketched above, gives rise to a dialectic between finiteness and facticity on the one hand, and transcendence on the other. On the one hand, the finite corporeal-spiritual beings discover that they are in *the* world together with other finite beings. On the other, they do not accept this ontic fact as such but try to give it an ontological meaning. This they do, not accidentally, but universally and of necessity. Thanks to their efforts to conceive the beings with whom they are together as an ontological whole and to structure that whole ontologically, worlds — in the plural — arise.

Because these efforts are, concretely speaking, made in different ways, these worlds manifest typical differences among themselves. Moreover, because the efforts of the corporeal-spiritual beings to give meaning to the totality of beings are subject to change, those materially and formally determined worlds are not stable phenomenological data. This point, however — and, more generally speaking, the problem of the dynamism of the worlds — will be dealt with in another lecture. Here we are primarily concerned with showing that a pluralistic view of the problem of worlds is a necessity.

A Priori World-Structures?

Let us think here once more of Husserl. As we saw, he is convinced that the knower can change his opinion concerning the existence or non-existence of individual worldly beings; he is also convinced that the structure of the world is and remains always the same. According to Husserl, the world-structures possess an *a priori* character, whereas the "world-content" is *a posteriori.*

Let us now consider the nature of those structures. Since, according to Husserl, they form the *a priori* guideline of the transcendental constitution of a world, he discusses them in the passages where he deals with the problem of universal constitution. It is in the second volume of his IDEAS that he most extensively characterizes the gradual constitution of the universe of being. His discussion shows that the structures of the world must of necessity comprehend spatio-temporal nature, animal nature, psychic reality, but also spiritual-personal reality.[1] According to the CARTESIAN MEDITATIONS, the constitutive theory must of necessity occupy itself with "the constitution of a spatial object (to say nothing of a nature as such), of psycho-physical being and humanity as such, culture as such."[2]

In his lectures about phenomenological psychology Husserl speaks at length about "the pervasive structure that belongs to the form of a world, and to a world as such."[3] Things, psychophysical realities, bodily, psychic and finally spiritual and cultural realities are named here as characteristic of the world as world of experience.[4] All those passages are more or less in agreement with one another.

The idea of the "everyday world" (*Lebenswelt*) introduces no changes in this. In fact, Husserl is convinced that the "everyday world" has "even pre-scientifically the 'same' structures as those that the objective sciences ... disclose as *a priori* structures in *a priori* sciences."[5] He gives causality as an example. The category of causality, Husserl believes, dominates also the thinking of the everyday world; the only thing that is missing there is theoretical idealization. Hence Gerhard Kluge gives the right interpretation of Husserl when he says that the

---

1. *Ideen*, vol II, *passim*.
2. "... Konstitution eines Raumgegenstandes und gar einer Natur überhaupt, der Animalität überhaupt, Kultur überhaupt..." *Cart Medit.*, p. 91; tr., p. 55.
3. "... durchgehende Struktur, die zur Form einer Welt und einer Welt überhaupt gehört..." *Phänomenologische Psychologie*, p. 103.
4. *Ibid.*, pp. 103-118.
5. "... Welt als Lebenswelt ... schon vorwissenschaftlich die 'gleichen' Strukturen [hat] als welche die objektiven Wissenschaften ... als apriorische Strukturen in apriorischen Wissenschaften entfalten." *Die Krise...*, p. 142.

everyday world "always already contains in itself the 'universal' which guarantees science."[6]

Martin Heidegger, too, uses a concept of structure as his guideline in his famous analysis of the phenomenon of worldliness. According to him, "world" corresponds to the structure of "care" (*Sorge*), *Dasein*'s familiar and "care-ful" dealing with beings. He sees the "world" as "that for which something 'ready-to-hand' of the surrounding world has been freed in such a manner that it becomes first of all accessible as a being-within-the-world."[7]

Both Husserl's and Heidegger's concepts of structure, however, give rise to doubts. Let us think, for instance, of the world of primitive man. For the primitive, the question concerning the fertility or infertility of worldly beings has an existential significance. The fertility of plants, animals and men depends on the favor of a demon of fertility. Thus the latter is, for primitive man, the most "real" being. But we ask ourselves to what ontological realm that demon belongs: to spatio-temporal nature, physical reality, or to the realm of spiritual-cultural beings? And we also ask whether we can look upon the demon's favor or his anger as causal operations which we can, in principle, determine, calculate and foretell.

More in particular, with respect to the "world structure" as described in BEING AND TIME, the following objection comes to mind. Has such a demon the mode of being of the *Dasein*, of a "ready-to-hand" or a "being-at-hand"? It is true that the principal "care" of the primitive is connected with discovering his exact relationship to the powers and forces of the cosmos. But his "care" is totally different from the "familiar and 'care-ful' dealing" with the "ready-to-hand." On the other hand, it is certain that the world of the primitive possesses a structure which is in harmony with the existence of magic powers that maintain the cosmos.

From this brief analysis we draw a threefold conclusion. First, it is evident once more that the material aspects of the world — the question about the worldly beings which we consider as real — are inevitably connected with the formal aspect — the question about the structure of the world. Secondly, we have ascertained how difficult it is to establish *a priori* laws about materially and formally determined worlds.[8] Thirdly, if we really desire to proceed in a truly phenomeno-

6. *Phänomenologie — Metaphysik oder Methode*, Bonn, 1966, p. 191.
7. "[Die Lebenswelt enthält] das Wissenschaft-verbürgende Allgemeine schon immer in sich." *Sein und Zeit*, p. 85.
8. Perhaps it is possible, by using a different road, to sketch ideal types of worlds without laying claim to *a priori* validity and completeness.

logical-descriptive way, we must hold fast just as much to the plurality and pluriformity of worlds as to the unicity of *the* world.[9]

Worlds, Particular Worlds, "Surrounding Worlds," Situations

If we understand this and desire to continue our phenomenological explorations, we will have to be very careful in our terminology. We will have to make the necessary distinctions and determine exactly what is meant by the ideas we intend to use in the following considerations.

In the preceding lecture we introduced and justified the distinction between *the* world as universal horizon for all and the materially and formally determined worlds. The everyday world, that is, the world prior to scientific objectification, is a particular type of such worlds,[10] and the world of the Western man of science is another type.

But it is not enough to make that distinction. When, for example, scientists speak of the "world of micro-organisms" and the "world of numbers," the concept "world" clearly does not have the same meaning. We have shown, to be sure, that then also there is question of a totality of beings, some of which are actually given and "an infinite number" of others are anticipated in the form of empty intentions. We find the typical principles of order and structures also in these cases. Yet, there is a difference; in fact, an essential difference. The formally and materially determined worlds spoken of above are something "in" which individual men and groups of men live. In other words, the materially and formally determined worlds essentially refer to the life of groups of people and that of individual men. It is not a coincidence that birth is referred to as a "coming into the world" and death as a "departure from the world." (For this reason, as we will see, a threat to his world can be for man a threat to his existence.)

All this has no application when I think of the "world of micro-organisms" or the "world of numbers." Both have a connection with

---

9. One gets the impression that Husserl was not blind to the pluriformity of world-structures. In an unpublished manuscript he tells us: "The 'form' of the world in which man ... lives ... is an individual form. Everyone who belongs to this world, that is, everyone who belongs to the same community as to my 'we' describes the same — and of necessity the same — individual form. A Chinese, insofar as he does not belong to it, describes another." Manuscript A V 5 of 1930, p. 96, quoted by R. Toulemont, "La spécificité du social d'après Husserl," *Cahiers internationaux de Sociologie*, vol. 24 (1958), p. 147: "Die 'Form' der Welt, in der der Mensch ... lebt ..., ist eine individuelle Form. Jeder dieser Welt Angehörige, d.h. jeder zur selben Gemeinschaft als die meinem Wir gehörige, beschreibt dieselbe und notwendig dieselbe Individualform. Ein Chinese, sofern er nicht zu ihr gehört, beschreibt eine andere."

10. For the problematics of the everyday world of life, see the author's *Phenomenology and the Human Sciences*, Pittsburgh, 1965, pp. 70-71.

my concrete life — this is sometimes forgotten by logical positivists — but it is a very special connection. The "world of micro-organisms" coincides with a whole of possible but not necessary experiences; the "world of numbers" agrees with a complex of typical conceivable notions. In such cases we shall speak of *particular worlds*. They arise for me by the fact that I proceed to transcend in one particular "direction" — for instance, through an anticipation of typical experiences — but not in all "directions" that are open to me. When there is question of complexes of pure conceivable notions, we will call them — somewhat in line with Husserl[12] — *particular ideal worlds* and thus distinguish them from *particular worlds of experience.*

The so-called *surrounding world" (Umwelt)* differs from these worlds. The surrounding world is connected with the life of individual subjects or groups of subjects. But it is a complex of concrete beings, really possible situations, really possible relationships — a complex that is not transcended. The surrounding world of a man is determined, for example, by the region he lives in, the social condition of the group to which he belongs, its means of production, etc. In contrast with the "world" there is here no transcending transition from what is really given or really attainable to the ideally conceivable or the ideally possible. For instance, the surrounding world is characterized by one or more landscapes, but not by all conceivable landscapes. Because the ability to transcend limits or boundaries is proper to man as a spiritual-corporeal being, we will speak of *worlds* only in relation to individual men and groups of people. Both man and animal, however, have their own particular surrounding worlds.

One could also say that the surrounding world of man and animal is determined by the totality of their really possible *situations*. This idea also plays an important role in phenomenological literature. To our thinking it is connected with an act of giving meaning, which causes a typical "constellation" of beings to appear; a "constellation" that issues from a particular function, from a way of acting. But a situation is not the framework of our whole life. We agree with Buytendijk when he says: "A situation is something which we find in a relation to our own existence and which has acquired a meaning by the act which constitutes as a situation that which has been found."[13]

Let us add that the statement, "The animal, too, lives in a surrounding world, the animal also knows and recognizes situations,"

11. With respect to the meaning of the particle "in" Heidegger offers some valuable indications in *Sein und Zeit*, pp. 52 ff., 130 ff.

12. Cf. *Ideen*, vol. I, p. 61.

13. Cf. *De Vrouw*, Utrecht, 10th ed., 1961, p. 94.

should not be understood in a naturalistic sense. We should not forget that "surrounding world" and "situation" are phenomenological notions; "environment," on the contrary, is a concept pertaining to natural science. It may be useful to explain this by means of an example. If I catch a bird and release it in my room to fly around there, we are both in the same environment, that is, the space, the shape of the room and the furniture, the temperature, the air pressure, the degree of humidity, the radiation and the stimuli that, in principle, can affect our senses, all these are the same for both of us. And yet it goes without saying that my situation and that of the bird are entirely different.

The surrounding world of a man, we saw, can be considered to be the totality of his really possible situations. Can we say something similar with respect to the relationship between "world" and "particular worlds"? Apparently not. For then we were exclusively dealing with real possibilities, but now we are speaking of real and ideal possibilities. We must, therefore, characterize the relationship between world and particular worlds in a different way. So we will say that the materially and formally determined world is the condition which makes the emergence and existence of particular worlds possible. Let us clarify this with an example. In a world in which thought is immediately connected with concrete activity, life or existence — for instance, the world of a primitive man — there is no room for a particular world of pure beings-of-thought, such as the "world of numbers."

Even more universal is the insight that the universal horizon of *the* world is the general and necessary condition for the genesis of materially and formally determined worlds. This we have already shown in the preceding lecture.[14]

2. How Is a "You" for "Me"?

Correct Formulation of the Question

Let us now return to our starting point. After gaining a certain understanding of the divergent concepts of "world," we now raise the decisive question, How does the "you" come into my world? Or more exactly expressed, How does the "you" take its typical place in the midst of a universe of beings-for-me that is materially and formally determined?

We have already prepared the answer. It consists in a radical negation of the assumption; in other words, the question is asked in the

14. Cf. above, pp. 37 ff.

wrong way. We do not hesitate to say: The "you" does not come into my world; it already is there, for the "you" is older than I.[15] More precisely speaking, we should say that the "you" is already a "you" with respect to me before I am an Ego. And I am an Ego only when there is a world for me. Later we will see what is concretely involved in this, but provisionally we must draw a negative conclusion from this insight. It is that the descriptions of some authors according to which one Ego suddenly become conscious of another Ego in the midst of his world cannot be called phenomenological. The situations which they describe do not correspond to any real experiences. This point, too, will later be discussed more in detail.

All difficulties, however, are not overcome because we have determined our standpoint. On the contrary; for now, with particular urgency, the following question forces itself upon our attention: If the "you" is already in the world, how then is it given to me? This question should not be understood solely in an epistemological or a practical sense. It does not mean in the first place, How do I know that a worldly being is a "you"? or, How can I as an Ego go about dealing with a "you"? What we are facing here is primarily an ontological problem; and that problem, correctly formulated, is, How does it happen that there is a "you" for me?

Understanding the "Tendency to Be"

This is an ancient problem, one that can be approached from different angles. The answer that comes most easily to mind has already been prepared in the preceding lecture. It is the ultimate unity of all worldly beings.[16] All are tied together, as De Waelhens says, by a common bond. All finite beings form a natural community within the universal horizon of the world. Like me, they, too, try to maintain themselves as beings. I understand their "tendency to be," their *conatus essendi,* as Spinoza calls it;[17] I understand that they are anxious and concerned with their being in the world;[18] I feel something like that linking me with them in a common lot.

If those worldly beings have a mode of being that is somewhat similar to mine, I understand them perhaps even better. I would then be inclined to apply to them the category of *Verstehen* (understanding) in the sense which Dilthey has introduced in the *Geisteswissenschaften* and which Buytendijk, Plessner and Merleau-Ponty have made familiar in modern psychology. Let us think, for instance, of the

---

15. Cf. above, pp. 29 ff.
16. Cf. above, p. 38.
17. *Ethica,* III, prop. 6.
18. *Sein und Zeit,* p. 187.

phenomenon of life. When we find an unknown kind of animal whose organs puzzle us from a morphological and functional standpoint, we nevertheless usually understand the situation in which the animal is, viz., we get the impression that it is fleeing or in pursuit of something, that it is feeding or hiding, defending itself or attacking something.

The one original situation of "we together in the world" branches out, as it were, into a series of particular situations which — at least, on the level of higher animal life — is open to an original understanding. The question how this can be explained in principle will be discussed later. For the time being it suffices to realize that I as a being in the world share the lot of other concrete finite beings and that this, in the first intance, makes it possible for me to turn to them.

The Intentional Turning to Others

The phenomenologist will be inclined to compare this conscious turning-to with the intentional directing of oneself to the other as other. This idea enables us to approach the problem of the "you" in a second way. For our analysis of the world as universal horizon makes it possible for us to indicate a fundamental feature of the intentional turning-to in general.

We may start from the "original situation" described above, viz., we together, surrounded by a universal horizon. It is true that the horizon of the world appears to be ultimately insurpassable. But it is primarily an "open" horizon, as we have said before. As such it invites exploration, expansion, enrichment. If I wish to expand my limited existence, I must direct myself toward other beings. For they are what I am not; they possess what I lack; they know what I don't know. Hence they can supplement what I in my finiteness do not possess. As a finite being, Heidegger emphasizes, I am dependent on other beings,[19] and the ontological ground of that dependence is the fact that the others are complementary with respect to me.

From this standpoint intentionality is nothing but my conscious entering into relationship with something or someone. The intentional "tending to" leads to satisfaction when my intentions are "fulfilled." This is ideally the case when the intended is immediately present to me. Thus it follows at once that we do not look upon intentionality as the expression of an impersonal or anonymous transcendental dynamism but, rather, as the expression of a primordial ontic desire for a bond with the other. This is a desire that cannot be satisfied by mere functions, activities, deeds and achievements. The presence of the other as other is usually obtained by openness, receptivity and suffering.

---

19. *Ibid.,* p. 87.

Intentional Turning-to or Transcendental Achievement?

As a third preparatory consideration, the concept of intentionality which we have developed here should be confronted with that of transcendental phenomenology. Why, one could ask, does our concept of intentionality differ so fundamentally from the transcendental-phenomenological concept? There are, we think, three reasons, which we will briefly describe here.

1. It is well-known that Husserl distinguishes two kinds of intentionality, viz., "act-intentionality" and "functioning intentionality." The first consists in the fact that consciousness is actively directed to its object; the second embraces all functions of consciousness which take place autonomously, such as, for example, the formation of associations. Such processes, which occur without any thematic knowledge or volition, Husserl calls "passive." In this sense he frequently speaks of "passive synthesis," "being affected" and "being temporalized." Ultimately, however, the functioning intentionality is connected with anonymous transcendental life. But this life, which ultimately seems to be the life of everything and everybody, can, in its turn, no longer be passive. For it is unique, all-embracing and absolute. It can in no way receive something from something else or undergo something through someone else, without ceasing to be transcendental. And so everything that in the natural attitude looks like passivity changes into transcendental activity, even into productive transcendental activity. For example, everything that has become temporalized owes its existence to the time-constituting stream of absolute subjectivity. It "arises" from the "original source" of that stream.[20] Hence transcendental subjectivity must be conceived as a wholly active spirit. Scheler has pointed out that it can be compared to the *Nous* of Averroes.

2. Let us for the moment leave aside this too speculative idea and confine ourselves to the act-intentionality. Even then our objection remains. For the act-intentionality is conceived as a mental tending-to. Now it stands to reason that a purely centripetal act of the mind — be it an act of knowing, striving or valuing — is incapable of calling into being a real relationship between two beings. Such an act can never explain how it happens that something or someone is present to me. To use a comparison, two searchlights shining upon each other are in no way connected with each other. In other words, even if the transcendental phenomenologist should be able to show that another Ego constitutes me precisely as I, through my intentional achievements,

---

20. *Zur Phänomenologie des inneren Zeitbewusztseins*, p. 75.

constitute the other Ego, even then it would remain most difficult to explain the simple phenomenon of my immediate being-with-the-other. Sartre's dialectic of the "look" draws the ultimate consequences from the doctrine ascribing a centrifugal character to intentionality.

3. A last source of objections lies in the fact that the historical Husserl has from the very beginning characterized the act-intentionality as objectivizing. The intentional act is directed to "its" object and not to anything else. This obviously makes it an enigma how one subject can be recognized as a subject by another subject. More generally speaking, we must say that transcendental phenomenology, by introducing the transcendental subject and the constituted object, has carried to extremes the tendency of Western philosophy to constantly increase the distance between subject and object. We ask ourselves whether such a way of looking at things does not lead to contradictions.

Generally and in principle it is necessary to realize this: if we understand by a subject a being that is exclusively active, and by an object a being that is purely passive, then no concrete relations between the two are conceivable. For in what would those relations consist? Every concrete activity — including every activity of knowing — demands, according to our experience, something that offers resistance to it. But where would that resistance come from? Every striving — including that for knowledge — overcomes obstacles to reach its purpose; thus, again, the possibility of resistance is presupposed. Only a Creator God, who give a creature being out of nothing, does not have to take any obstacle into account. Hence it is not by accident that the subject-object relationship has been changed into a productive relationship in transcendental phenomenology, and that it has issued into a "nihilating" relationship in Sartre's existential phenomenology. The evidence which Martin Buber has emphatically brought forward that every relation demands reciprocity[21] has not been set off to full advantage.

What Is Presence?

It is true that Buber's valuable idea needs further philosophical development. If we call "presence" not co-existence in space nor simultaneity in time, but the being of a concrete reality insofar as it is near me, accessible to me, close to me, in short, insofar as it *is* together with me, then three formal principles are to be applied to that fundamental relationship.

---

21. "Ich und Du," *Schriften zur Philosophie, Werke,* vol. I, Munich, 1962, p. 88.

First of all, it is evident that I cannot be present to this real being unless it is present to me. With Buber, one can call this most general principle the "principle of reciprocity."[22]

Secondly, a modal rule corresponds to this ontological principle, viz., the way I am present to a real being is universally and of necessity attuned to the way this being is present to me.

Thirdly, an analogous rule applies with respect to the dynamism of the finite beings that are present to one another. This rule may be expressed as follows: the way I "deal" with a real being is generally and of necessity attuned to the way this being "deals" with me.

To avoid a fundamental misunderstanding, let us note at once that a reciprocal relationship is not necessarily symmetrical. For example, the way a father is present to his son is not the same as the way the son is present to the father; the way a teacher deals with a pupil differs from the way the pupil deals with the teacher. Buber himself clearly expressed this point.[23] The modal principles merely say that both modes are not independent of one another, that they are related to one another, fit in with one another. Otherwise it would be impossible for two beings to enter into a relationship with one another.

The three principles formulated above apply not only to conscious beings, acting persons or people who talk with one another. They are not only valid with respect to dialogue in the narrow sense, but have an ontological significance. Let us show this through a brief analysis. Buber says that "work, activity is a 'one-sided' procedure. There is a power in the midst of the person; from there it goes forth and implants itself into matter.[24] We disagree with this restriction of the principle of reciprocity. The matter of which Buber is speaking is concretely a particular kind of material that lends itself to a particular way of being shaped because of its properties and structure. The sculptor, for example, takes the nature of his material into account. He choose his materials in view of the work he intends to do. Thus the relationship is in no way a one-sided relationship.

What has been said here of a practical relationship can also be applied to a cognitive relationship. Eugen Fink has pointed this out. The being that can be known does not merely refer to itself but also presents itself to the knower. "Being," Fink says, "goes out of itself when it appears, when it makes its appearance."[25] More concretely

---

22. *Ibid.*, pp. 82, 85, 88, 129, 163. Buber sometimes also speaks of "Mutualität."

23. "Reden über Erziehung," *Werke,* vol. 1, p. 806.

24. "Werkhaftes Tun ist ein 'einseitiger' Vorgang. Da ist eine Kraft in der Mitte der Person, da geht sie aus, bildet sich dem Stoff ein ... " *Ibid.,* p. 791.

25. "Das Seiende geht von sich selbst her auf, wenn es erscheint, zum Vorschein kommt." *Sein, Wahrheit, Welt,* The Hague, 1958, p. 102.

we could say this: if, for example, a thing which we wish to observe did not manifest itself, was invisible to us and could not be reached by our sight, we would be unable to know it. Hence, when the thing manifests itself, it is in a certain sense a "cooperating" object.

If this is the way things are generally and of necessity, we should not hesitate to draw the necessary conclusions, but we should do that carefully and systematically. A first negative conclusion is easy to formulate: we must renounce the idea of an absolute subject and of an object that exists only thanks to that subject. Such an idea contradicts all our self-experience and our experience of other reality. We have no experience whatsoever of a pure activity or of a totally unresisting passivity. Insofar as my being with concrete beings is dynamic, it takes the form of an active-passive interplay. This interplay can be such that sometimes the roles of subject and of object are interchangeable. More exactly expressed, the "relative" subject — that is, the subject who is predominantly active in a particular respect — can also become a relative object; reversely, the "relative" object — that is, the object which is predominantly passive in a particular relationship — can also become a relative subject.

Let us clarify this rather complicated matter by means of an analysis. On purpose we will select as the topic of our analysis a relationship that is typical for our life of perception. To avoid complications, let us imagine that the human race had only one sense faculty at its disposal, namely, the sense of touch. In other words, those human beings are blind, deaf, and lack also sensations of taste and smell. The only way they can arrive at knowledge of reality and of one another is though tactile impressions.

Those subjects will, of course, go around with extended arms and sensitively outstretched fingers. This means that there is question here of an "empty" anticipation; they count in advance on the possibility that "there is something"; they run ahead of experience. Let us now suppose that two of these blind people bump into each other. They make contact by way of collision. The blind men then know only that "there is something." This shows that perception is not a contact, although it begins with a contact.

How can these two blind men arrive at a perception after their first collision? The answer cannot be that both at the same time execute movements with their whole bodies, for in this way neither of them would acquire any knowledge. To make progress in knowledge, it is evidently necessary that there be a tacit understanding between them. One will touch, the other will allow himself to be touched; one will execute movements of touch, the other will remain relatively motionless; one will perceive, the other will allow himself to be perceived. After that, they will exchange roles. This is the only way those two people can learn to know each other.

This example is most instructive for us. The one blind man evidently "plays" the part of a subject, the other that of an object of knowledge. The "object" is not indifferent, insensitive, apathetic. He cooperates in bringing about the perception by undergoing something, by exercising patience, by remaining motionless. This is his way of "manifesting" himself or, as Fink expresses it, "of making his appearance." When, next, the two exchange roles, the one who was a subject now plays the role of an object, and the one who was an object now becomes a subject.

From this we must draw an important philosophical conclusion, viz., that no immutable ontological characteristics correspond to being-a-subjct and being-an-object. A being can function now as a relative subject and then again as a relative object, according to what is demanded by communication. Only one law governs that interplay, viz., the law of reciprocity in the sense we have defined above.

This is not a new insight. When Hegel says that the interplay of powers consists "in those opposite determinations of both, their being for one another in that determination and the absolute, immediate exchange of determinations,"[26] he offers us a phenomenologically justified characterization of the nature of dynamic relations between two concrete beings. At the same time, it is clear that the image of the interplay between powers is an "example" of the interplay between things that are dialogally related to each other. Before developing this point further, however, we must discuss a serious difficulty.

3. The Problem of Thinkability (Cogitabilitas)

We are thinking here of an objection that is to be expected from the side of transcendental phenomenologists. Our critique of transcendental phenomenology, they would tell us, is beside the point, it is an "expedition into alien territory." All our descriptions were concerned with relationships between concrete beings, but Husserl as well as Sartre speak of an essentially different kind of relationship.

With respect to Husserl, they argue, his very reduction "bracketed" all beings and he merely asked where the reality comes from which those beings that are changed into phenomena claim for themselves. But the law of intentionality applies here, that is, the phenomenal objects of which I am conscious correspond exclusively to particular

---

26. " ... in diesem entgegengesetzten Bestimmtsein beider, ihrem Füreinandersein in dieser Bestimmung und der absoluten unmittelbaren Verwechslung der Bestimmungen ... " *Phänomenologie des Geistes*, ed. by G. Lasson, Leipzig, 2nd ed., 1921, p. 92.

acts and functions of my consciousness. They are nothing but *noe-mata* called to life by particular *noeses*. Thus my consciousness is not conceived as a reality but as that upon which all reality-for-me is based. It is only in this transcendental sense that consciousness is a subject; only in this transcendental sense is the whole of reality in all its articulations an object. Husserl himself expresses that fundamental idea in the formula: "I think the things that are thought" (*Ego cogito cogitata*).

We will omit here the objections that can be raised against the idea of a "pure consciousness." As the existential phenomenologists have already pointed out, through the transcendental-phenomenological purification consciousness is divorced from the human body; together with the body, the connection with a situation, a surrounding world and a materially and formally determined world, also becomes a victim of the transcendental-phenomenological reduction. It is difficult to accept such an acosmic, ahistorical and asocial consciousness — in other words, a consciousness that does not dwell in a world.

It is not our intention to discuss once more those objections, which have been voiced, for example, by Merleau-Ponty. Instead, we want to say something about Husserl's own *cogito*. As is well known, Husserl corrected and completed Descartes' *Ego cogito*. No one who is familiar with the development of modern Western philosophy doubts the fact that Husserl thereby made a great step forward. Yet it is possible that even the new formula is not entirely satisfactory. For it lends itself to two interpretations. First, it could be taken to merely express a correlative relationship. *Ego cogito cogitatum* would then mean, "I intend" (*Ich meine*) and to my intentions *corresponds* "that which is intended" (*das Gemeinte*). If this is the meaning of the formula, it has no world-shaking import, for it then merely points to a formal correspondence.

Secondly, it could also be true that Husserl's *cogito* expresses a creative relationship. It would then mean this: I intend and from my intending — and from nothing else — the intended comes forth. In this interpretation the formula affirms something that cannot be shown in any self-experience or that of something else. But such an assertion would conflict with the spirit of Husserl's entire work, to the extent that his work is descriptive in nature.

Let us ask ourselves, therefore, more precisely what is really meant by *cogitatum*. What exactly is "the thing intended"? The usual answer is that the *cogitatum* is the object meant, the matter I have grasped and in the way I have grasped it. Yet the formula *ego cogito cogitatum* cannot mean that from my "intending" there comes forth the perfectly grasped matter, as Pallas Athena with her armor issued from the head of Zeus. If this were what the formula is supposed to express, then no constitutive analysis would be possible. Thus Husserl's discussions of sense *hyle* and intentional *morphe*, of passive synthesis and identifying syntheses, of "layers" and phases of the constituting act would be incomprehensible. The genetic aspect of his phenomenology would collapse.

If, on the contrary, constitution is the historical process of giving meaning, then something precedes the understanding of the matter; and it does not precede accidentally but necessarily. Then the *cogitatum* is not first in the process of giving meaning, but last. That is why, I think, we must formulate a principle which lies at the foundation of the *cogito* — the Cartesian as well as the Husserlian *cogito* — and which, consequently, must be considered to be more fundamental. This principle is: *Ego cogito cogitabile,* I think the thinkable.

The Existential Ground of the Cogito

The formulation of this principle inevitably raises a new series of questions, questions that are primarily concerned with the exact sense of that formula. Does it indicate a formal correlation or a creative relationship? Does our new *cogito* mean a return to realism? Must the "thinkable" be conceived as a reality in the sense of naturalism, a reality which somehow "casuses" my *cogito*?

All this is far removed from our intentions. We believe that the problem of thinkability is more fundamental than all realistic or idealistic interpretations of Descartes' fundamental idea. It includes the ontological problem that we left aside in our preparatory considerations. Did we not say, at the beginning of this chapter, that the finite beings in the world are bound together in a common "fate," that they have a "tendency to be" which we understand, and a common original situation? Did we not speak of turning-to, relationship and dealing-with? We are convinced that all such concepts are provisionally empty of any content; they are merely references to problems as are Heidegger's *Dasein*-with and Jaspers' co-existence. All of them presuppose something that is very elementary and yet still needs to be shown — namely, that there is at least one factical being that is the same way I am and that, in that pregnant sense, "is with me."

The term "factical" is of the greatest importance here. It does not refer to conceivable things, essences, eidetic possibilities, but to an existential certainty. As long as I do not have that certainty, all the above-mentioned concepts float in the vacuum of metaphysical thought-spinning. How can I know that the beings around me have a "fate," that they tend to maintain themselves in existence, that they find themselves in a situation? Why should I turn to them, enter into relations with them, deal with them? Who tells that "presence" is more than a nice-sounding word? Who guarantees that the being of the others is in fact the same as my being? As long as this is not clarified, the possibility of the *cogito* and of thinkability remains a riddle.

Our question, then is concerned with the ground on which the possibility of the *cogito* is based. Obviously we should not look for this ground in another *cogito*, for that would lead us into an endless series. To avoid that series, we must ask ourselves whether there exists a presence that is not that of a *cogitatum* to a *cogito,* but something that is eminently present, something that justifies all tending-to-or thinking-of, an "original presence" that makes possible the intentional turning-to and is a guarantee for the thinkability of the world.

Life teaches me that there must be a presence which is not — not primarily — a thought of my thinking, that there is a being which is "originally present" to me. There is a first thinkable, a *primum cogitabile*. All of us know it and in our daily life we have a name for it. We call it "you." But let us note that the "you" is not a specimen of the species *homo sapiens*. What sort of "species" the "you" is and what characteristics its representatives exhibit is something we know on the basis of our objectifying experience. The "you" is not grasped in the same way as an object; more exactly expressed, to the extent that the "you" is fully you, it escapes objectifying experience. *The "you" is "believed."* The term "believed" obviously does not have here the same meaning it has in a theological discourse or in the philosophy of Hume. By "belief" or "faith" we mean an affirmation of reality which in its inmost nature is independent of objectifying knowledge.[27]

In that sense, my affirmation of the "you" must transcend all doubt for me; it must be characterized as the "primordial faith" (*Urdoxa*) upon which all my further *cogito's* rest. For the nearness of the "you" is a primordial presence, one that makes me believe that relations with other beings also are meaningful. My turning-to a "you" is the most elementary turning-to, one that causes my intentionality to awaken. In short, only the "you" makes me be an "I." That is why, we repeat, the "you" is always older than the "I."

This principle holds for every aspect and all levels of human life. Husserl speaks of primordial faith in connection with the "being given" of the things that are experienced.[28] It is precisely through the mediation of a "you" that I know at all that there are things worth touching, tasting, looking at, listening to. A "you" teaches me also that there exists reality which can be manipulated, "utensils" destined

---

27. We will return to this provisional description. Cf. p. 118.
28. *Ideen,* vol. I, p. 256.

for a particular use (Heidegger), matter which I must modify in my work (Marx). Without the active-receptive interplay with a "you" I would not know that my existence has a social dimension (Merleau-Ponty). In short, to the typical question of transcendental phenomenology, How is the "you" given to me?, we should like to answer once again by a denial of the assumption. The "you" is not *given* to me but is a *giver* for me; and because it is a giver for me, it is "believed" by me.

Let us now return again to Husserl. We know that Husserl in the fifth CARTESIAN MEDITATION tried to explain the nature of intersubjectivity in a transcendental-phenomenological way. This attempt has been the subject of suspicion, criticism and rejection. Of the numerous attacks perhaps that of Alfred Schütz is the most competent because it is based on a perfect understanding of the problems faced by Husserl.[29]

Husserl tries to deduce the reality of the other Ego from the reality of perceived nature. In fact, however, just the opposite is true. Nature is essentially nature-for-us; the "you" points out to me that there is for us a nature that can be explored through perception and that can be practically conquered. We must even go further and say that a perfectly solitary, finite consciousness would be a dormant consciousness. That which makes me to an awake, conscious and self-conscious Ego is a "you." In other words, conscious beings would not be able to be conscious without one another. They stand to one another in a relationship of reciprocity, as was clearly seen by M. Nédoncelle.[30] To our mind, it is precisely on this point that the fundamental idea of dialogue offers a corrective that can help phenomenological philosophy overcome its impasse.

What Is a Finite Cogito?

The price that must be paid for appropriating the dialogal vision is the renunciation of deeply ingrained habits of thought. This has already been shown by the preceding considerations. But there is one point that we wish to bring up here explicitly for discussion. If the *cogito* is no longer the work of a unique, solitary, all-embracing consciousness, then it is a finite *cogito;* there is no other alternative. The existential phenomenologists have already understood this. They discovered that the body, perception and language are indispensable conditions. They pointed out that the act of thinking has a worldly character, that

<hr/>

29. "The Problem of Transcendental Intersubjectivity," *Collected Papers,* vol. 3, pp. 51-83.
30. *La réciprocité des consciences,* Paris, 1942.

it is historically and socially conditioned. Merleau-Ponty, in particu-
ular, has done pioneer work in this respect.[31] And yet his considerations, we think, need to be made more complete.

Let us first establish in general what we mean by a finite *cogito*. In
Lecture One we showed that the finiteness of our thinking cannot
arise from a self-limitation. This is impossible because thinking, while
conceiving a limit, thinks at the same time of that which is beyond
this limit. Yet our *cogito* is finite; and it is finite because, while thinking, it calls up horizons of thinking. In other words, it leads to a thinking that has no definite content, to a grasping-by-anticipation that is no
longer a grasping-of-something. It is in this sense that the human
cogito must be called finite.

Such general considerations, however, do not suffice. They do not
answer the justified question of the phenomenologist, How does that
finiteness show itself? But we are now sufficiently prepared to face
that problem. In the spirit of our previous reflections we can say that
the finiteness of our consciousness manifests itself in a threefold form.

First, this finiteness appears as a universal horizon, which announces
by its "no" that the "I am" of my *cogito* is not the "To Be," *tout court,*
and this *cogito* cannot lay claim to transcendentality.

Secondly, the *cogito*'s finiteness manifests itself by the fact that it
cannot be without being a "response" to someone or something; and
this being-a-response is wholly different from simply "implying" another *cogito*. This means that my "thinking" — no matter what one may
mean by it — is never a sovereign act. I cannot think without attuning
the mode of my thinking to that which must be thought. But because
the "you" is the "first thinkable" (*primum cogitabile*), I must in the
first place attune my thinking to the being of the "you." We may even
say that, generally speaking, my thinking comes about because there
is a "you" that thinks and invites me to a thinking "response." It is
this "you" that makes it clear to me for the first time that thinking is
possible and meaningful. This also shows the finite, social and historical character of my *cogito*.

Thirdly, my *cogito* is finite because of necessity it goes on to constitute a world together with the "you." More carefully expressed, this
means that I attune my thinking to the thinking of a "you" in such a
way that we conceive and transcend the totality of given beings in the
same "style." If this were not the case, we would not live in a common
materially and formally determined world. I and you then could
never become a "we."

---

31. See the chapter *Le Cogito* in *Phénoménologie de la perception,* pp. 423-
468.

On the other hand, being-attuned-to does not mean the same thing as completely conforming-to. The common material and formal determination of the world for us does not at all have to be total or invariable, but is concerned only with the general "style" of conceiving and transcending.

What Husserl already suspected[32] and what the existential phenomenologists have stressed, is a phenomenal datum that cannot be denied, namely, there is always a certain tension between the world-for-me, this individual, and the world for the concrete "we" to which I belong. This is also in accord with what we have shown above. The way I, as conditioned by my bodily, social, historical and personal conditions, turn to beings is ultimately unique. This uniqueness, however, may not be absolutized; it is only relative. For it delineates itself against the background of a turning-to-reality that is typical of a group, a class or a people at a particular historical time. The "individual world-form" spoken of by Husserl is, therefore, only a more or less divergent variant of a communal world-form. This statement applies in principle also to the world of the genius, the hero, the revolutionary or the religious reformer. Their *cogito*, too is not unique in the absolute sense of the term.

4. Dialogal Constitution

What Is Dialogue?

The reader must have noticed that our idea of constitution differs from that of the transcendental phenomenologists and that our notion of dialogue also deviates from that of dialogal philosophy. We must therefore clarify these two fundamental concepts.

Let us begin with the second and think of Martin Buber as a typical dialogal philosopher. His principal work, I AND THOU, presents itself from the very first line as a philosophy of speech, the word, or language. This is not surprising if one consider the "climate" in which Buber lived and developed his ideas. We must ask ourselves, however, whether such an approach takes the diverse levels of human existence sufficiently into account. No one today doubts that between the "I" and the "you" there can exist relations which not only remain verbally unexpressed but which are also of themselves nameless, "anonymous." We are thinking here in particular of the emotional-corporeal and of the practical levels of interplay between "I" and "you." These levels are not merely important from the standpoint of genetic and comparative anthropology; they also play a role in the life of the mature and civilized man, where they function as a background that now and then can become a foreground.

32. Cf. above, p. 49, footnote 9.

This means that we must broaden the concept of dialogue. It comprises not only communication by means of symbolic sounds but every form of reciprocal communication between subjects. In line with what we have said before,[33] we will speak of dialogal being when my presence to a "you" is attuned to the presence of a "you" to me. A dynamic definition corresponds to this ontological-static description: dialogue as an active-receptive interplay makes its appearance when my way of "dealing" with a "you" is attuned to the way the "you" "deals" with me. This dealing-with can exhibit a pre-rational character; it can take place in wordless way; it can rest upon one body-subject's understanding of another body-subject.[34] Yet, such cases also are, we think, steps and levels of a dialogal way of being.

Three remarks must be made to prevent a misunderstanding of the definitions we have just given. First, let us repeat the warning that reciprocity is not symmetry and that being-attuned-to does not mean conforming-to.

Secondly, the dialogal partner mentioned in our definition is the "you," in the sense described in the preceding reflections upon "the first thinkable." We thereby wish to convey that a dialogue with a "you" is the original image and exemplar of "the" dialogue. The way a "you" can become *the* other, and the other can become *an* other for me should be extensively described in a phenomenology of social life.[35] Our definitions do not exclude but include such variants of the dialogue.

Thirdly, it must be pointed out that being-attuned-to is not the same as being-harmoniously-attuned-to. On the contrary, without tensions, differences of opinion, divergencies of practical and theoretical approaches, the dialogue would soon come to a standstill. A "you" that cannot contradict the other cannot really speak with him. Moreover, opposition, enmity and conflict belong to the fundamental ways in which I can deal with a "you"; they are part and parcel of the dialogue. These ways must be among the main themes of a social philosophy that wishes to be called phenomenological.

What Is Constitution?

After this explanation it is no longer difficult to draw the much-debated concept of constitution from the semidarkness of transcenden-

---

33. Cf. above, pp. 17 ff., 21f.
34. For the concept "body-subject" in Merleau-Ponty see Remy C. Kwant, *The Phenomenological Philosophy of Merlean-Ponty*, Pittsburgh, 1963, pp. 11 ff.
35. See, for example, Karl Löwith, *Das Individuum in der Rolls des Mitmenschen*, Darmstadt, 2nd ed., 1962; Michael Theunissen, *Der Andere*, Berlin, 1965.

tal idealism and expose it to phenomenological daylight. To constitute does not mean for us to endow a meaningless *hyle* with a meaningful *morphe*. If the nature of intentionality consisted in that, the intentional turning-to would remain a riddle.[36] Neither can constitution mean that the meaning of being is given to something which does not exist. For that would be a kind of idealism, an "idealism of giving meaning," as one philosopher has expressed it.[37]

To constitute, on the contrary, is a continuous process of giving an ever clearer meaning; it is, as De Waelhens once said, "a promotion of meaning." That is why the expression "to *give* meaning" should never be understood in an absolute sense. The giving of meaning never starts from absolute zero; it never magically calls forth the meaningful from the absolutely meaningless; it is never creative in the absolute sense of this term. For the world as universal horizon, the others, and our materially and formally determined world are always co-constituents when I proceed to an act of giving meaning.

The process of giving meaning passes through various stages. The first of these we could perhaps call the emotional-corporeal stage. Through the bodily needs and the biological drives and dreads, there arises a first meaningful structure in the "landscape" that surrounds us. These needs and drives are grasped by other spiritual-corporeal and purely corporeal subjects through the body's expressiveness, and they lead to a first understanding.

A subsequent stage is characterized by the ability to deal with various "things to be handled" through position, movement and conquest of space. Here the structure of the surrounding world[38] is determined by the phenomena of "nearby" and "far away," "before" and "behind," "easy" and "difficult." Others not only perceive my practical behavior but, while perceiving it, they also understand it. In this way there arises a practical understanding that makes it possible for us to deal with one another, to play together and to work together.

Among spiritual-corporeal beings also a first objectivity is assured when a being can be known and recognized by all the members of a concrete "we" as being the same.[39] In other words, the thinking as such of something as the same must be made possible for all and by all members. This can be accomplished only by means of language. Hence the process of constitution is completed through the meaningful and

---

36. Cf. above, p. 45 and below, p. 102 ff.
37. We owe this expression to our regretted colleague J. A. Peters.
38. Cf., for example, F. Buytendijk, *Algemene theorie der menselijke houding en beweging,* Utrecht, 1957.
39. See the chapter "The Objectivity of the Everyday World" in our work, *Phenomenology and the Human Sciences,* Pittsburgh, 1963, pp. 65-87.

consistent application of a language-sign to one and the same thing. For this reason we must say that something is constituted by us and for us when the meaning we give to it is "sealed" through our giving it a name. Only then is there question of an "intentional pole," a focal point, that is, the very same being to which all can orient themselves in the same way, be it emotionally, practically, cognitively, etc.

Demythologization of Phenomenology

The object of our endeavor in all this is now perhaps clear. It is to demythologize phenomenology. The concept of constitution may serve as an example. More, however, is involved than merely trying to give clarification of this concept. We admit, of course, that such a clarification is badly needed. Eugen Fink, for example, discovered that Husserl used the technical term "constitution" in four different senses.[40]

More important is the fact that within the framework of a dialogal phenomenology the questions concerning the "who," the "how" and the "when" of the act of constituting can be raised, although the answer is not always simple and unambiguous. To the question, Who constitutes?, we will have to answer in the first instance, "we." "We" means here not only I, you, the others, our socio-economic and historical way of living and working together, but also our bodies, our world, *the* world. In other words, pre-personal realities also are involved in the process. One could therefore be inclined to give preference to the formula, "*It* constitutes itself but not without us," or more exactly, "It constitutes itself, but the final decisive giving of meaning is reserved to us as personal beings."

The "how" of constitution also takes place in and by the dialogue on all levels that dialogue can have. Dialogue is never the work of a solitary consciousness, one that refers only to itself. And in this way the question concerning the "when" is also answered. Constitution is continuously taking place in our dialogal existence. But it can be considered complete when a being is fully taken up into our discourse, that is, when all of us can speak about it, albeit in diverse ways, as the same.

Demythologization and Mystery

All this, we realize, means a break with the ancient tradition of a philosophy of immanence and reflection. If our view is right, then constitution does not occur in the mysterious interiority of an Ego

---

40. "Les concepts opératoires dans la phénoménologie de Husserl," *Husserl,* Cahiers de Royaumont, Philosophie, no. III, Paris, 1959, pp. 214-240.

that can never be adequately known by another Ego. Constitution is
not the work of a society of monads whose mode of being is enigmatic.
It does not flow from a transcendental Consciousnes that is the consciousness of no one and of nothing. But constitution takes place before our eyes, in the clear daylight of our corporeal-spiritual, social
and historical life. It also has aspects that can be studied by physiolo-
gy, psychology, sociology, anthropology and history.

In spite of this, constitution remains no less myserious. For not one
expert in the above-mentioned sciences can tell us how it is that
"worldliness," bodily being, sociality and historicity are intertwined
in an original way in our constituting of meaning. The novelty of
dialogal philosophy consists perhaps in this that the mystery lies no
longer in a world behind the world; it does not hide behind the
reality of bodies, sense data, or socio-historical processes. The mystery
occurs among us, near us and, to some extent, through us. One who
believes in what he sees and reflects on what he believes sees also the
mystery. On the other hand, one who has no confidence in what he
sees but believes in theories, systems and models, one who only reflects
upon his own thought-constructs, will never encounter the mystery.
What he meets is meaninglessness.

LECTURE FOUR

THE GROWTH OF AWARENESS*

1. Knowing the Other Ego

Introductory Remarks

No one has ever doubted that man is able to know and recognize his fellowmen. As a matter of fact, man finds that very easy. He does not look upon it as an achievement comparable to that of estimating distances or solving chess problems. Knowing or recognizing the other Ego happens "very naturally" without any effort. But *how* this happens we do not know. Generations of philosophers and psychologists have made mighty efforts to offer intricate theoretical explanations of something that in actual practice seems very simple. Names that come spontaneously to mind here are, for example, John Stuart Mill,[1] Ferdinand Avenarius,[2] Theodor Lipps,[3] Edmund Husserl[4] Max Scheler,[5] the Gestalt psychologists, Jean-Paul Sartre,[6] Norman Malcolm,[7] and Alfred J. Ayer.[8] These authors have presented the most penetrating arguments, and their theories are in many respects very interesting. But none of them gives any explanation of what really ought to be explained.

It is impossible for us to review here the opinions of those philosophers and psychologists. All we intend to do is prove by means of some examples that they did not solve the heart of the problem, viz., the knowing of the other Ego as an other Ego. There is certainly some truth in Lipps's claim that man, through a primary instinct, knows the inner life of other individuals and shares their intimate experiences. But the question is why that primary instinct operates with re-

---

*We prefer to use here the term "awareness" rather than "consciousness" because deep-rooted prejudices connect a more or less explicit *self*-consciousness with the notion of consciousness.

1. *An Examination of Sir William Hamilton's Philosophy*, London, 6th ed., 1889, pp. 243 f.

2. *Der menschliche Weltbegriff*, Leipzig, 3rd ed., 1912.

3. "Das Wissen von fremden Ichen," *Psychologische Untersuchungen*, vol. I, Leipzig, 1907, pp. 94-222.

4. *Cart. Medit., pp.* 121-177.

5. *Wesen und Formen der Sympathie*, Frankfurt a.M., 5th ed., 1948.

6. *L'être et le Néant*, pp. 275-367.

7. "Knowledge of Other Minds," *Essays in Philosophical Psychology*, ed. by Donald A. Gustafson, New York, 1964, pp. 365-376.

8. "One's Knowledge of Other Minds," *ibid.*, pp. 346-364.

spect to certain beings and not in reference to others. Why can I emphatize with other men but not with cybernetic machines?

Scheler, no doubt, saw something important when he pointed to the phenomenon of sympathy. And yet it is incomprehensible why I sympathize with another Ego but not with any other kind of organism. Similarly, the fact that the other man appears as a Gestalt is accepted by almost all psychologists. But a tree and a triangle also appear to us as Gestalts. Thus the question remains how the other Ego's Gestalt differs from other Gestalts.

When we read the above-mentioned authors and study their theories, we cannot avoid the impression that they are all dealing with the same question, that they differ only in their way of thinking and their language, but fail to arrive at a decisive answer. There is scarcely any progress toward a solution.

Merleau-Ponty's Concept of the "Body-subject"

One exception must be made to that lack of progress in philosophical anthropology, and this exception is Merleau-Ponty. He is the first thinker — and until the present the only one — who has critically examined the terms in which the crucial problem has always been expressed. Merleau-Ponty asks himself what is really meant by "the problem of the other Ego." The other Ego refers to a being that conceives itself as a consciousness, just as I myself am primarily a consciousness; and with respect to the latter, every one continues to cling to the trusted Cartesian pattern of thought, whether one calls oneself a neo-Kantian, a transcendental-phenomenological thinker, a psychologist of consciousness, or an existential philosopher. In other words, philosophers look upon the Ego as a consciousness that knows itself by means of reflection; they hold, moreover, that the intimate knowledge which the Ego has of its own inner consciousness differs essentially from the knowledge of things, nature and the world. One of Merleau-Ponty's great merits is that he dared to challenge those seemingly self-evident assumptions.

Is it really true that I conceive myself primarily as a consciousness, that is, as an interiority of consciousness which is perfectly transparent to itself, to its own reflection? This Merleau-Ponty most firmly denies. He holds that I conceive myself primarily as a "grip upon the world," as a being which through perception orientates itself and practically behaves in a world. The perceptual as well as the practical intentions are meaningful and meaning-giving from the standpoint of my existence. Yet this meaning does not start with a mental consciousness but with an Ego-body. This Ego-body that is not yet personal — and in this sense purely "natural" — is the origin of the perceiving, motoric, elementary-practical, sexual and expressive intentions. That is why Merleau-Ponty speaks of a *body-subject*, which is neither consciousness nor a thing, but manifests a "third way of being.[9]

With this a step forward has truly been taken with respect to our problem. For if I conceive myself primarily as a being that deals with worldly realities, that behaves practically in various situations, that lends a biological meaning to things and situations, I conceive the other body-subject in the same way. In other words, when I perceive a being that flees or defends itself, that hides or feeds, then I understand those ways of behaving "from within" and recognize the being in question as another body-subject. There is then between me and the other the possiblility of a certain communication on the practical-biological level.

Merleau-Ponty's new model of thinking can help us up to this point but not further. As he himself adds, another body-subject is by no means another Ego.[10] Spiritual consciousness also belongs to another Ego, and how do I know that the other body-subject has a spiritual consciousness? To explain this, Merleau-Ponty has recourse to an explanation of Husserl: the body of the other Ego is present thanks to my perception; the consciousness of the other Ego is "ap-presented" thanks to an association with the body that is perceived.[11] The foundation of this association lies in the fact that my own consciousness has an intimate connection with this functioning body-subject. But this line of thought leads us once more into the Cartesian alley. And at once the typical doubts reappear. Why do I "ap-present" a consciousness when I perceive certain body-subjects rather than others? Why, for example, do I conceive a snake and a spider as body-subjects but not as other Egos? Merleau-Ponty points out in passing that a body-subject deals with natural objects whereas another Ego deals with cultural objects.[12] But this is not a satisfactory explanation. The problem is merely displaced by it, for the old question now returns in a new garment: How do I recognize cultural objects as cultural objects?

We believe, therefore, that we must look for a solution in the spirit of Merleau-Ponty, but not in accord with his words.

Determination of the Points of Departure

Let us return to our starting point. When something is very simple

---

9. *Phénoménologie de la Perception*, Parts One and Two, in particular the chapter "Autrui et le monde humain," pp. 398-421.

10. *Ibid.*, p. 37.

11. Cf. *Cart. Medit.*, par. 50-54, pp. 138-149; *Phénoménologie de le Perception*, pp. 409, 415.

12. *Phénoménologie de la Perception*, p. 407.

in actual practice but very puzzling in the theory that tries to explain it, one cannot help suspecting that there must be something wrong with the theory. In the case we are considering here there is no need to look for logical errors, but we must seriously envisage the possibility that perhaps the philosophical "language" in which the problem has been expressed is not appropriate.

The language in which philosophers speak with themselves, with one another, or against one another is historically conditioned. A historian will find it strange that the problem of the other Ego played no role at all in ancient and medieval philosophy, but appeared only in modern times. As is well-known, Descartes is held to be the Father of modern philosophy, and rightly so. He has exercised considerable influence, even upon those who opposed him. Thus one would suspect that Descartes and the philosophers influenced by him used concepts and categories which made this problem insoluble. It is not difficult to show that this is actually the case. The formulation of two typical theses of Cartesian or Cartesian-inspired thought suffices to show the consequences that flow from them with respect to our problem.

The first of these two theses is: the Ego is the subject of thoughts, conscious acts (*cogitationes*). There are great differences in the way that being-a-subject can be conceived. Descartes speaks of a "thinking substance"; Locke of an "inner world"; Kant of an "I think" that accompanies all my conscious acts; Husserl of an "Ego pole" from which all objectifying intentions arise. The thesis can, of course, also be reversed, that is, one can also say that the subject of conscious acts is an Ego. From a negative point of view one may then maintain that something which is not a subject of conscious acts is not an Ego.

The second thesis is: every Ego has, through reflection, access to its own thoughts or conscious acts. Here, too, the proposition can be reversed to read: that to which I have access through reflection is my own thoughts.

Once these premises are accepted, there is no escape from the conclusion that no Ego has access to another Ego. But the question is, of course, whether those presuppositions are true. And to this we vigorously answer in the negative. In order to put our own idea of the Ego and its thoughts in the sharpest contrast with the Cartesian concept, we will formulate here five propositions which we consider to be provisional starting points with respect to the question of knowledge of other Egos.

1. Awareness is not a "substantial" subject of functions, acts and intentions, but is the way-of-being of an Ego.

2. The way-of-being which we call awareness is not immutable but changeable; it can assume different forms.

3. An Ego can be aware without having an explicit self-awareness. In this case the Ego does not reflect upon itself.

4. An Ego can be aware without being intentionally orientated toward objects.

5. The non-intentional, non-objectifying awareness is, considered from a genetic standpoint, the oldest form of awareness.

This is not all, however. We must distinguish two different aspects in the mutability of awareness. They are concerned with, in the first place, the mutual, essentially different forms of awareness, such as an objectifying and a non-objectifying awareness; in the second place, they refer to the varying degrees of being-aware, of which unawareness is the lower limit. In connection with these degrees we should think of purely dynamic relations. What has been traditionally conceived as a static being-aware is, if closely considered, a continuous process of becoming aware, followed by becoming unaware. We are dealing here with the most inconstant, volatile and "vulnerable" mode of being. This alone suffices to brand as misleading the traditional image of awareness as an imperturbable stream that flows in only one direction. If a metaphor is to be used, one should rather speak of a fire that smolders, flares up in flames, spreads light and heat for some time, and then dies out.

All such images, however, are not of much assistance to the philosopher. As phenomenologists, we must look for the precise meaning of those images. We must ask ourselves, What is the basis of our claims? Are they not purely speculative? What experiences do we have with respect to the Ego's becoming aware and becoming unaware?

Becoming Aware and Becoming Unaware

Actually, there is a superabundance of experiences. The most common of these is that of becoming less aware because of fatigue. Let us say that, while writing, my attention begins to slip. I notice this because I confuse concepts which I ought to distinguish very sharply and because I am unable to establish a connection even when the relationship is evident. I am "distracted," unable to concentrate. More accurately expressed, I have lost my firm grip on objects in my world — in this case, on the concepts of my particular philosophical world. As a result, I am unable to play the old game of "uniting" and "dividing" as is demanded by the laws of logic. If, according to Merleau-Ponty, attention is the power of awareness to dominate a mental field,[13] a lessening of attention because of fatigue expresses itself in the disorganization of my mental "landscape."

---

13. *Ibid.*, p. 37.

Another kind of becoming unaware that is also an everyday experience is falling asleep. Husserl has philosophized about "the blank of sleep" (*Schlaflücke*) in many of his unpublished manuscripts. Waking-up from sleep also could be a topic of phenomenological descriptions.

For our problem, however, such descriptions would be of little value. Let us consider the case of waking-up. When I wake up from a profound sleep, I recall in a flash what happened to me yesterday. The familiar situations of my surrounding world emerge one after the other and with them also the horizons of my world. This statement applies even more to the phenomenon of a passing fatigue, like the one described above in which I lose my grip on the orderly concatenation of the objects of my study. I quickly recover and, once more, have them firmly in my grasp. In both cases becoming aware takes place rapidly and easily, without difficulties or detours, because I can base myself on acquired knowledge, my mental possessions — my "habitualities," as Husserl would express it — and because, on the other hand, my objectifying functions have already developed and acquired experience.

But all this is not the way in which we would be able to establish the theses we have formulated above. In our theses there was question of a non-objectifying awareness, which is genetically the oldest form of being-aware; moreover, in the preceding chapters we referred to the primordial presence of a "you." We maintain that the intentional and objectifying orientation of the Ego toward a surrounding world and toward a world corresponds to a later phase of becoming aware and that this phase is preceded by a long and difficult development. To prove this, we should, as Paul Ricoeur expresses it, proceed to an "archeology of the subject."[14] We should trace the genesis of the Ego and its active-receptive interplay with persons and things. Who was I, I should ask myself, before I became a mature man who is experienced in objectifying thought and inclined to reflection? Which beings existed formerly for me? How were they given to me? These questions would have to be answered with respect to my whole life from my birth until now. In short, we would have to survey the entire ontogenesis of my awareness.

Difficulties of Method

The difficulties we meet here may seem insuperable. It is impossible for me to recall the process of my development, and the reason obviously is that forgetting belongs as much to my awareness as does learning. Once again, being aware is really a matter of becoming aware

---

14. *De l'interprétation*, Paris, 1965, pp. 407 ff.

and becoming unaware; and to our becoming unaware of particular contents we give the name of "forgetting."

The greatest difficulty, however, lies in this that, if our theses are valid, my former way of being-in-the-world was essentially different from my present way; for instance, my way of being involved with persons and things during my early childhood was totally different from my present way. Now, as we saw in Lecture One, it can happen that such earlier typical experiences are "buried" in the course of my development. We saw that in fact my development failed to come to a standstill only because an older layer of experiences was "covered over." In this respect, as we have shown, the reflective and retrospective effort of the phenomenologists is useless.[15]

Ricoeur points out that, fundamentally, my birth is for me as mysterious and unapproachable as is my death.[16] But what he says about my birth is equally applicable to my first experiences, my first turning to persons and things, the first explorations of my life. They can be compared to ancient geological layers that are buried under numerous layers of new rock formations having an entirely different structure. I will never be able, as my own "archeologist," to lay bare, through my own efforts, the oldest formations of myself.

The transcendental phenomenologist comes to the end of his tether here. He will never be able to describe the genesis of being-aware, nor the genesis of a "we," nor be able to reconstruct the coming-to-before-us of a world. The dialogal phenomenologist, however, is not limited to the resources of reflection and retrospection. His methodology is essentially different, for he can have a dialogue with a "you." He can turn to others who are older than himself and who have carefully and systematically observed his development.

With a clear conscience he can do what phenomenologists such as Scheler, Merleau-Ponty, Ricoeur, Buytendijk and Plessner have done before him: he can enter into a dialogue with experts in the sciences of experience. For these experts have compared, critically sifted and put in order the insights and discoveries achieved by many others in a particular field. They represent the state of knowledge of a concrete "we," which with Husserl may be called a "community of research." With respect to our problem, then, we shall not hesitate to enter into a dialogue with the experts in the sciences of experience and, more particularly, with psychologists who have made a systematic study of the development of human awareness.

---

15. Cf. above, p. 17.
16. *Philosophie de la volonté*, Paris, n.d., pp. 407 ff.

Philosophical Reflection upon Empirical Data

We realize, of course, that our interest in the results of developmental psychology can be misinterpreted. For this reason we will begin by eliminating certain misunderstandings. First of all, we reject the view that psychology is the fundamental discipline underlying the totality of all sciences, including philosophy and logic. We are familiar with the absurd consequences drawn from so-called "psychologism" in the nineteenth century.

Secondly, it is not our intention to create a new psychology in a speculative fashion. We recognize psychology as an empirical science and realize that whatever is affirmed or denied in the realm of psychology must be justified by empirical methods. Philosophical constructs would be entirely out of place there.

It is for this reason that we consider the psychologist as an autonomous partner in the "dialogue of seekers of truth." In our opinion, the psychologist has his own special contribution to make to this dialogue, and this contribution is of an empirical nature. On the other hand, we ascribe to ourselves the right and even the duty to reflect upon the relatively certain results of modern psychology.

The relativity and historical character of this certainty do not deter us. We acknowledge that we are children of the twentieth century and that we reflect upon the scientific insights of our time — just as Aristotle, Aquinas, Kant and Husserl have done in their time. In principle, we would agree with Alphonse de Waelhens's thesis that philosophy is a reflection upon a non-philosophical experience."[17]

At the same time, emphasis should be put on the fact that the philosopher's reflection upon the results of empirical sience is philosophical. His reflection is neither empirical nor anti-empirical; it lies in a different dimension, viz., that of philosophy. If, then, we frequently appeal to the findings of psychologists in this lecture, this appeal should not be misunderstood. By numerous quotations we wish to show two things: 1. negatively, that we are not trying to create a developmental psychology through unsubstantiated *a priori* deductions; 2. positively, that we are really speaking here of relatively certain results attained by modern psychology.

Finally, our appeal to psychological data does not at all mean the abandonment of our conviction that ultimately reality has a mysterious character. The final lecture of this book will make that very clear. For the present we will limit ourselves to the remark that the modern view of what a mystery is does not militate against a reflection upon

17. *La philosophie et les expériences naturelles*, The Hague, 1961, p. 2.

the sober results of the empirical sciences. If, for example, genetic psychology concretely reveals the genesis and bloom, the fading and final decay of human lives, it offers us an opportunity for a philosophical reflection which can lead to an encounter with the mystery. The question whether genetic psychologists know this or not, will it or not, is, in the first instance, of little importance. The decisive element here is the spirit in which we as philosophers reflect upon the results attained by the psychologists.

2. How Does Becoming Aware Originate?

Thus we ask here the unheard-of question, How does being become being-aware? And, in reference to our first thesis, this means, How does an Ego become aware? Even this formulation is still ambiguous. It must be interpreted in the spirit of our third and fourth theses, in the following way: How does an Ego finally arrive at relating itself to a world of real and possible objects as well as to itself? What development precedes this? And how does this development begin?

Of course, we must take into account that for a child, at first, there exist only real objects; that he knows only a limited number of situations and only a limited number of typical modes of behavior — in other words, that the child lives in a surrounding world but not yet in a world.[18] But the situations known by the small child are interconnected in a particular meaningful way, a way that is typical for the structure of the relevant surrounding world. Our task will consist, in part, in determining the nature of that structure.

Let us note that we are not concerned here with the first reactions of the neonate or with the objects to which he reacts. Such problems belong primarily to the physiologist. Because the concept "reaction" has a vast extension and a small comprehension, it can also have a chemical and physical sense. Lifeless matter also reacts. What interests us here, however, is the question whether and when the child grasps something in the framework of a situation, whether and when he notices the interconnection of situations. Only then can it be said that there is question of "perceiving" in the proper sense of the term, of "conceiving" and "giving meaning."

a. THE PRE-OBJECTIVE STEP OF DEVELOPMENT

The first thing that should attract the thinker's attention is the fact that a child is born of a mother. And yet, to my knowledge, among all philosophers, only Martin Buber has taken the trouble to dwell, however briefly, upon that fact.[19] What does it mean, philosophically speak-

---

18. Cf. above, pp. 66 f.
19. *Werke,* vol. I, pp. 94 f.

ing, that a man "comes into the world" only through another human being? Doesn't this fact alone establish once and for all the facticity of his dialogal existence, his lack of autonomy, his being orientated to a "you" that is older than himself? As we will see, this initial physiological bond with the mother influences the development of the child, not only physiologically but also psychologically.

It is also interesting to note that the infant spends most of his first few weeks in a sleeping condition. As Heinz Remplein expresses it, the first two months of a child's life are "the age of sleep."[20] For one who sleeps without dreaming there exists neither a world nor a surrounding world. As long as the infant is asleep, he notices no objects, has no desires and does not tend to anything. He does not devise meaningful structures, he does not "stand out" toward intentional poles, he does not project a world. He preserves and safeguards his frail existence by withdrawing into unawareness. Sleep is his "endeavor to be."

To the extent that the infant is not sleeping, there is truly a certain tending-to. This tending-to, however, does not have an objectifying character. To understand what this technical expression means, let us think first of the cognitive sector of the infant's life. In this sector the infant does not perceive any "objects" in the proper sense of the term. Psychologists are in agreement that the neonate reacts to all kinds of sense stimuli but is not able to arrange his impressions in an orderly fashion.

Paul H. Mussen, for instance, writes: "Even though a neonate's sense organs function relatively well, it seems unlikely that he *perceives* the world as adults do. Perception involves the organization and interpretation of simple sense impressions."[21] The Dutch psychologist Alphons Chorus tells us: "Immediately after birth the neonate can hear, see, smell and feel. Hence sound, light, hardness, softness, wetness and dryness, all these qualities reach him, but at first all this does not yet 'say' anything to him; it has not yet a *meaning* for him; he even finds it annoying. He is still unable to take up and assimilate the outside world with its sounds, colors and impressions, He is even afraid of it."[22] René Spitz goes even further when he writes: "There is no differentiation between incoming stimuli; and the behaviour which

20. *Die seelische Entwicklung des Menschen im Kindes- und Jugendalter,* Munich, 14th ed., 1966, pp. 126-155. Hereafter abbreviated as *Entwicklung.*
21. *The Psychological Development of the Child,* Englewood Cliffs, N.J., 4th ed., 1964, pp. 19 and 32. Hereafter abbreviated as *Child.*
22. *Zuigeling and Kleuter,* 10th ed., Haarlem, n.d., p. 27. Hereafter abbreviated as *Zuigeling.*

takes place seemingly in response to these stimuli appears to be un-specific."[23]

The Primacy of the Subject-Subject Relationship

It follows from this that the first structuring of the surrounding world cannot be based upon perceptions. But is such a structuring then possible at all? Don't we know since Aristotle that all concepts of reality ultimately rest on sense data? The newborn child may not be able to assimilate and develop sense impressions in such a way that they give him objective knowledge; nevertheless, he is endowed by nature with a certain equipment. He is filled with biological longings and dreads. If those longings and dreads were mere physical forces, they would of course not be a source of meaning. But, in accord with our dialogal view, they are expressions of the fundamental dimensions of this young life, viz., its being-orientated-to and its knowing-itself-to-be-threatened.

These two aspects demand to be completed positively and negatively; they demand something that satisfies the biological longings and averts biological dreads. In our general philosophical considerations we called this complement of the needy Ego, the "you." In reference to the little child, the "you" will normally be the mother in our Western civilization.

To the infant the mother is not given as an object having a particular size or color; rather, she appears in a threefold form. She is, first of all, one who brings pleasure, delight, satisfaction; secondly, she guarantees security; and thirdly, she holds power over the surrounding world.

Numerous psychologists have observed the first two of these motherly roles. Mussen, for example, writes: "Typically, the mother gratifies the infant's primary needs for food, for alleviation of pain, and perhaps even for tactile stimulation . . . Many of these satisfactions are provided as she feeds the baby."[24] And Chorus adds that the mother "is a being who makes a child share in all kinds of gifts; from her come warmth, food, ease, pleasant dryness and such a nice succession of laughter and babbling sounds."[25]

With respect to keeping in check biological dreads, L. Joseph Stone and Joseph Church refer to Liddell's experiments on animals. These showed that certain actions which in little lambs and kids usually produce an artificial neurosis remained ineffective when the young ani-

23. *A Genetic Field Theory of Ego Formation*, New York, 1959, p. 15. Here-after abbreviated as *Genetic Field* . . . .
24. *Child*, p. 66.
25. *Zuigeling*, p. 44; cf. also *Entwicklung*, pp. 147, 183.

mals were with their mothers.[26] And Remplein remarks: "The presence of the mother seems to counteract the appearance of dread. A child that is seated on his mother's lap feels secure."[27]

Now, a mother would not be "a being who makes a child share in all kinds of gifts" if she did not have any power. It is true, of course, that the concrete meaning of this power is understood by the child only in the next stage of his development, the practical-objective stage. But even as an infant, the child established a connection between the appearance of the mother on the one hand, and being-satisfied, put-down-dry, plunged-into-a-warm-bath, and being-freed-from-pain, on the other. One who can satisfy gnawing hunger, remove unpleasant wetness, or change pain into pleasure is powerful. The question how mother can do this does not yet arise in the baby's mind.

It is understandable, therefore, that this generous, protective and powerful being is the first one that the child knows and recognizes. In other words, it is this being which the child seizes as a particular being before any other thing, any natural object, any cultural object. About this matter all psychologists are in agreement. W. Metzger has written most extensively about this topic. To quote him, "The 'Mother' is that 'Something' in whose presence everything becomes good. Often as early as the second week, the child begins to distinguish not only the voice but also the visible figure of that Something from other, similar voices and figures. In the course of the second month the focussing of the eyes and the organization of what is seen generally has progressed so much that this Something acquires a face — even if at first only when there is a front-view and an erect position — and the eyes are the center of that face. This is the time when the child beings to respond with a smile to mother's glance."[28]

Remplein reports practically the same facts and adds to them:

---

26. H.S. Liddell, "Conditioning and Emotions," *Twentieth Century Bestiary*, New York, 1955, pp. 189-208.

27. "Die Anwesenheit der Mutter scheint dem Auftreten der Angst entgegenzuwirken. Auf dem Schosz sitzend fühlt sich das Kind sicher." *Entwicklung*, p. 183.

28. " 'Mutter' ist das Etwas, bei dem alles gut wird. Schon von der zweiten Woche ab beginnt vielfach neben der Stimme auch die sichtbare Gestalt dieses Etwas sich von anderen - gleichgültigen - Stimmen und Gestalten zu unterscheiden. Im Verlauf des 2. Monats scheint im allgemeinen die Scharfeinstellung des Auges und die Durchgestaltung des Gesehenen so weit fortgeschritten zu sein, das dieses Etwas, wenn auch zunächts nur in Vorderansicht und aufrechter Stellung ein Gesicht bekomnt, mit den Augen als Schwerpunkt. Es ist die Zeit, wo das Kind den Blick mit Lächeln zu erwidern beginnt." "Die Entwicklung der Erkenntnisprozesse," *Entwicklungspsychologie*, ed. by H. Thomae, Göttingen, 1959, p. 422. Metzger mentions in his contribution studies made by Charlotte Bühler, Dix and Meili-Dvoretzki.

"Smiling occurs first in relation to human beings. . . . It indicates a contact-making that is at first reactive and later on active. . . . The turning-to-the-world of things is achieved only at a later time."[29] Similarly Wilhelm Hansen remarks: "It also belongs to the condition of the child that he enters into contact with man before he is able to deal with things."[30]

Chorus elaborates the point in this way: "What is easier to perceive, a dot, a ball, a cube or a face? The last-named is, no doubt, the most complicated . . . A colored spot a child can more easily perceive than a ball; a ball is more easily apprehended than a cube. This we are inclined to think as mature persons, but it happens not to be true for a child. A child knows much earlier the face of a human being; a child reacts much earlier to the face of his mother than to a colored spot and to a ball."[31]

Spitz speaks in this connection of a "pre-objective apprehension": "The establishment of the precursor of the object certainly is preceded by increasingly organized responses to the ministrations of the environment, represented by the mother. . . . This process culminates in . . . the emergence of the smiling response, which represents a conscious, reciprocal communication."[32]

Physiognomic Perception

If we were to ask how, in these cases, the mother is given to the little child, our question would really be misleading. For in phenomenological terminology "being given" refers to the appearance of an intentional object to a subject. But it is an established fact that the mother is present to the child in a pre-objective way. It is true, of course, that we grown-ups find it most difficult to conceive that primitive mode of presence. For this reason we will refer here to an experiment with animals that can shed light on the matter.

Harry Harlow, of the University of Wisconsin, "put newly born monkeys with 'mothers' made from wiremesh. . . . Some were fed from a bottle attached to the chest of an unadorned wire 'mother,' while the 'mother' of the others was made of wiremesh, but covered

---

29. "Das Lächeln erfolgt zuerst im mitmenschlichen Bezug. . . . Es stellt eine anfänglich reaktive, später aktive Kontaktaufnahme dar. . . . Die Hinwendung zur dinglichen Welt vollzieht sich später." *Entwicklung,* p. 156.

30. "Mit der besonderen Lage des Kindes hängt es auch zusammen, dasz es bereits zum Menschen Kontakt findet, noch bevor es imstande ist, mit Dingen etwas anzufangen." *Die Entwicklung des kindlichen Weltbildes,* Munich, 6th ed., 1965, p. 148. Hereafter abbreviated as *Weltbildes.*

31. *Zuigeling,* p. 46.

32. *Genetic Field* . . . , p. 18.

with terry cloth material. The latter structure thus supplied both
food and a great deal of tactile stimulation whereas the former gave
food but not the same quantity or quality of tactile stimulation. Giv-
en the choice of going to either 'mother,' baby monkeys characteristically preferred the terry cloth one and spent more time clinging to
her than to the other one, even those babies originally fed by the plain
wiremesh 'mother.' When a frightening wooden spider was placed in
the cage with a young monkey, he would run to the terry cloth 'mother,' who was apparently the more effective source of security." Mussen, to whom we owe that account of Harlow's experiments, con-
cludes with these words: "The experimenter concluded that tactile
stimulation is innately satisfying to an infant animal, so he forms a
strong attachment to whatever or whoever offers it."[33]

Harlow's conclusion, however, is not very satisfactory. Let us suppose that the experimenter had made use of a real bird-eating spider
instead of the wooden substitute. The live spider, no doubt, would
have been able to give to the little monkey tactile sensations of a remarkable kind from both the quantitative and the qualitative standpoint. Why, then, does the little monkey not attach itself to the spider? Why does he run away from it? Why does the spider inspire
dread when the monkey has not yet had any experience with spiders?
And what has the feeling of security given by the terry cloth "mother" to do with tactile impressions?

The stimulus-response pattern leaves us stranded here. For the
fright-inspiring impression of the spider on the little monkey we have
to appeal to the idea of "physiognomic perception," which Heinz
Werner has introduced in modern psychology.[34] But there is another
idea that plays an important role in Werner's work and that can be
useful here, viz., the idea of the "syncretic character of primitive organization."[35] In reference to the terry cloth "mother" in Harlow's
experiment we can say that softness, warmth, nearness, gentleness and
security belong together in the experience of the young monkey; and
they do the same in the experience of the young child. There is question here of "signal properties," in the sense given to this term by Werner. Where softness and warmth are predominant, there one can cud-
dle and there one feels safe.

The wiremesh "mother" does not possess the two first-named qualities. That is why she is also less loved as a nurse, and safety is in no
way expected from her. It is, moreover, worth noting that softness,

---

33. *Child*, pp. 68 f.
34. *Comparative Psychology of Mental Development*, rev. ed., Chicago, 1948,
pp. 67 ff. Hereafter abbreviated as *Comparative*.
35. *Ibid.*, pp. 59 ff.

warmth, nearness, gentleness and security do not form a syncretic whole *only* in the primitive apperception of baby monkeys; on the contrary, this is also true of man, as is evidenced in the highest forms of poetry, including religious poetry. Perhaps we are dealing here not merely with signal properties but with qualities that have become — and this not by sheer coincidence — deeply felt symbols for the whole of mankind.

The Role of Feeling

Let us return to the question of how the mother is present to the infant. To describe this, we must make use of the word "to feel." All the meanings of this term — and they are numerous — apply here. "To feel" has a reference to tactile impressions; it also applies to other sense perceptions that require nearness, such as experiencing warmth. Thirdly, the subject feels himself; for example, the baby feels comfortable, satiated, secure. He feels his own condition, but — and this is a new point of view — he feels it in his contact and through his contact with his mother. His feelings change completely when this contact is absent. The baby feels safe because he feels his mother. Hence we must say, fifthly, that the infant and mother feel themselves as one. But this should not be taken to mean that the affective unity is formed only by two individuals who are isolated from their surroundings. In fact, the situation and even the entire surrounding world are "felt" as peaceful, pleasant and safe; this, then, is the sixth meaning of the term "to feel."

Remplein rightly remarks that "feeling does not merely totalize a man but also binds him with his fellowman into a higher unity. Even in grown-ups the tonality of feeling is experientially coupled with the wealth of expression and the coherence of the surrounding world. This applies all the more so to a child, which is very characteristically an 'affective being'."[36]

Inquiring about the common meaning of all these semantic variations, we find no better expression than that of Helmuth Plessner to characterize feeling; he calls it "distance-less coherence with the matter."[37] Our preceding analyses can perhaps clarify what Plessner means by that "being immediately connected with the matter itself," or "consciousness of a contact that excludes all distance." "To feel" as such is, in its most original form, the opposite of intentional aiming at something; the latter always implies a "distance" between the

---

36. *Entwicklung*, p. 185.
37. ". . . distanzlose Sachverhaftung." *Lachen und Weinen*, Bern, 2nd ed., 1950, p. 173.

subject who intends and the intended object. This "distance," however, should not be exclusively understood in a spatial sense. "Distance-less" primarily means that there is no intermediary between the
one who feels and that which is felt; there is no question yet of the
typical tension between subject and object, but the feeling subject
feels himself by the fact that he feels his fellow-subject. Reversely, the
fellow-subject who is felt is present to the feeling subject by the fact
that the latter feels himself.[38]

Awareness Without Ego-awareness

Thus it is not surprising that the infant has no Ego-awareness in
the proper sense of the term. More accurately expressed, he does not
yet clearly distinguish the "I" from the "we." As Chorus writes: "The
individual and certainly the child are not autarkic; they live and can
develop only in a human community. The child does not live as an
'I' but lives in a 'we,' in a common bond with his whole surroundings.
And that 'we' of the child is formed first and foremost by the human
beings around him."[39] Spitz speaks of reciprocal object-relations that
always take place within the dyad of the child and his libidinous object.[40] Remplein assures us that the social relations of an infant
should not be compared to those between adults. "Above all," he says,
"there is lacking the split between I and you that gives a characteristic
tension to the experience of the adults. The 'I' and 'you' are still
encompassed by the wholly undivided unity of the 'we-experience.'
This is particularly true of the original form of contact with fellowman, namely, the relationship between mother and child."[41]

All this explains why the attitudes, behavior and emotions of his
parents, the nature of which is incomprehensible to the child, nevertheless exercise an influence upon the child's life. According to Remplein, "It is incontrovertible that the child's unconscious reacts like a
sensitive seismograph to the unconscious standpoints, attitudes and
prejudices of his parents. He responds to the parents' calm and the

---

38. We have stressed the necessity to introduce the concept "pre-intentional
level" into psychological theory in a previous work, *Das Gemüt*, Freiburg i.Br.,
1956, pp. 128-141.
39. *Zuigeling*, p. 46.
40. *Nein und Ja. Die Ursprünge der menschlichen Kommunikation*, Stuttgart, 1957, pp. 54 f. Hereafter abbreviated as *Nein und Ja*. What Spitz, in
psychoanalytic terminology, calls "the libidinous object" we characterize as
"fellow subject."
41. "Vor allem fehlt die Spaltung in Ich und Du, die dem Erleben des
Erwachsenen eine eigenartige Spannung verleiht. Ich und Du gehen noch in
völlig ungeschiedener Einheit im 'Wir-Erleben' auf. Dies trifft besonders für die
Urform des mitmenschlichen Kontakts, die Mutter-Kind-Beziehung zu." *Entwicklung*, p. 184.

security, their harmony and joy of life, as well as their irritability and
anxiety, their discord and tempers."[42] The term "contagion of feeling" (Scheler)[43] can be applied to this phenomenon. This expression
points to the fact that the process of "contagion" takes place outside
the conscious Egos.

According to Hansen, the mother is the first representative of the
surrounding world for the child. The way the surrounding world presents itself to the child depends on the reciprocal relationships of feeling.[44] We should like to understand Hansen's words in the sense that
the mother is an intermediary between the child and his surrounding
world. Because the infant is unable to take care of himself, it depends
on his mother whether his biological longings will be satisfied or frus-
trated. Hence the mother is in no way exclusively an object of love,
as eighteenth century sentimental writers would have us believe. She
can also arouse other emotions.

The mother's "help gives rise to satisfaction, his 'love,' " Chorus
tells us in reference to the little child, "but the other side, the mother's
refusal, provokes anger, his 'hatred.' And no doubt in those experiences lies the inducement for the division of the child's tendencies into
love and hatred, likes and dislikes. We say that the child is ambivalent
in his striving; this means that love and hatred will easily turn into
their opposites."[45]

The mother who gives herself awakens libidinous feelings and joy;
the mother who refuses provokes anger and hatred; the mother who
turns to someone else arouses jealousy. St. Augustine remark in this
matter is well-known: one infant is jealous when another is being
nursed. If a mother ill-treats her child, if she does not calm his anxieties, if she withdraws completely from him, his vitality may be crip-
pled. The experiments of Erik Erikson[46] and René Spitz point in that
direction. Paul Mussen writes: "Infant reared in emotionally cold and
unstimulating environments — for example, institutions, where they
are cared for routinely and without individual attention — tend to be
quiet, passive, inactive, unhappy, and emotionally disturbed." [47]

---

42. " . . . steht es unumstöszlich fest, dasz das Unbewuszte des Kindes auf
unbewuszte Einstellungen, Haltungen und Fehlhaltungen der Eltern wie ein
feinster Seismograph reagiert. Es beantwortet Ruhe und Sicherheit, Harmonie
und Lebensfreude der Eltern ebenso wie ihre Reizbarkeit und Aengstliechkeit,
ihre Zerwürfnisse und Launen." *Ibid.*, p. 215.

43. *Wesen und Formen der Sympathie*, p. 11.

44. *Weltbildes*, p. 39.

45. *Zuigeling*, p. 51.

46. "The Course of Health Personality Development," *The Adolescent — A
Book of Readings*, ed. by J.M. Seidman, New York, 1960, p. 219.

47. *Child*, p. 67.

Emotion as a Primitive Reaction

The mother's behavior can arouse in her child all the emotions known to us. And since the circumstances of life of a baby are simple compared to those of an adult, it may be useful to ask here what is meant by the term "emotion." It is certainly not synonymous with "drive" or "need." Hunger, thirst, pain and need of sleep can *cause* emotions, but they themselves are not emotions. Neither is an emotion a "motive." A motive is often based upon intellectual considerations and leads to coolly intended actions, which is not the case with emotions. Emotional behavior is immediately recognizable as such, as is the typically emotional apprehension of a situation and of the surrounding world. The last-named point is incomprehensible if we accept Jean Piaget's opinion that "the energy source of behavior belongs to affectivity whereas the structures belong to cognitive functions."[48]

If we wish to understand why emotional behavior can so easily be recognized, three characteristics of emotion should be mentioned.

1. Emotions always appear in connection with situations which, to use a modern expression, are existential in nature. An infant, for example, is angry, not because he is hungry but because he feels that his existence is threatened. No one can make it clear to the child that he will not die of hunger and that mother is all set to give him food. He feels a biological need. Similarly, dread in a small child is a feeling of being threatened by the unknown, the strange. By this it differs from fear, which is aroused by the perception of a typical danger and which we should call an "affect" rather than an "emotion."

2. An emotional behavior is eruptive and expressive in nature. That is why one notices it immediately. From a negative standpoint this implies that a person who behaves emotionally does not act on the basis of reflection, of the discovery of good reasons, the weighing of motives. Similarly, he does not look for the proper means or the most appropriate series of measures that will enable him to attain a well-defined end. That is why the cultured adult has the impression of passivity when he is overpowered by an emotion.[49]

3. An emotion is a primitive form of reaction on the part of a subject. We meet an emotion when a subject sees his surrounding world or his situation not by way of objectifying it, but immediately in the

---

48. " . . . l'énergique de la conduite relève de l'affectivité tandis que les structures relèvent des fonctions cognitives." *Les relations entre l'affectivité et l'intelligence dans le développement mental de l'enfant*, Paris, 1954, p. 5. Hereafter abbreviated as *Les relations*.

49. Cf. R.S. Peters, "Emotions, Passivity and the Place of Freud's Theory in Psychology," *Scientific Psychology*, ed. by B.B. Wolman and E. Nagel, New York, 1965, pp. 365-383.

light of existential needs and dreads. This is mostly the case with a little child. But the adult can always return to such elementary forms of behavior when his existence is endangered, whether really or only apparently. His desire, his need, his longing, his dread are then so great that they overcome him. In such occasions, the "original distance" that characterizes man[50] and that enables him to determine his attitude with respect to fellow-subjects, things and situations, vanishes. And the objective world constibuted by him as a grown-up also loses its meaning.

The consequences flowing from emotions have already been traced to some extent in the preceding paragraphs. The man who is in the grip of an emotion acts without consideration and deliberation. He neglects to make use of the proper means or to follow a reasonable path. He does not judge things "with a cool head." Hence there is a lack of orientation when the man who is the prey of emotion begins to act. A good example of this is the so-called "panic flight," studied by René Dejean.[51] It is also well known that the man who fights in a fit of anger runs the risk of becoming the loser when his opponent is cold-blooded and has a technical fighting ability. On the other hand, emotion can also appear as an outburst of biological energies capable of overawing and deterring a primitive adversary.

Emotional Dimensions

The above-described conception of emotion is connected with our conviction that a pre-objective structure lies at the foundation of man's existence, that is, a structure which is not based on objectifying knowledge and discerning volition, but which springs forth from biological impulses. Hence this structure cannot be described in terms of objects, nor of goals and purposes, but only by indicating the emotional high marks and low marks. Such high and low marks are characteristic of an "emotional dimension."

We want to link our reflections here with our analysis of the infant's early experiences in reference to his mother. The mother, we saw, normally brings pleasure and relieves pain; she occasions joy and removes feelings of dread; she is powerful and helps the child who feels powerless. If she fails to do this, anger and hatred well up in the child. In line with this analysis we should like to distinguish three fundamental emotional tendencies:

1. The inborn desire for pleasure and that of turning against the one who puts an obstacle in the way of satisfying that craving.

---

50. Cf. Martin Buber, "Urdistanz und Beziehung," *Werke*, vol. I, pp. 411-423.
51. *L'émotion*, Paris, 1938.

2. The innate need for security, and aversion for what causes dread.

3. The desire for power and the tendency to overcome powerlessness. These two manifest themselves only at the practical objectifying stage of the child's development.

We should like to designate the three emotional dimensions by the Latin terms *libido, securitas* and *potestas*. In actual behavior these three dimensions are characterized by the following contrasting pairs: the high points of love versus hatred, joy versus anguish, triumph versus despair.

All these ideas must, of course, be conceived in an analogous way. For example, the libidinous satisfaction of an infant obviously, even at its highest point, cannot be compared to the paroxysm of love in an adult lover; similarly, the despair of a toddler greatly differs from that of a guilt-ridden criminal. Yet one can rightly speak here, we think, of an analogy, for the adult who reaches those high points or low points returns to the level of emotional behavior that can easily be recognized as such.

This theory of emotional dimensions also offers an explanation of the typical ambivalence of emotional feelings. This ambivalence is well known today through Eugen Bleuler's studies in psychopathology. As we saw, however, this ambivalence also plays a role in a normal child and a normal adult. Why does love so quickly and so easily change into hatred, elation into disheartedness, triumphant feeling of superiority into a depressive feeling of inferiority? There must be some structure that lies at the foundation of this ambivalence. That is the reason why we cannot accept the view of Piaget, who postulates that a structure is always cognitive in nature. This postulate is the result of his very one-sided definition of the concept "structure."[52]

It is not our intention to claim that we have presented here a brand-new theory of the emotions. The significance of the first two emotional dimensions — *libido* and *securitas* — were discovered by psychoanalysis and that of *potestas* by individual psychology. We also agree with the teaching of both schools of depth psychology that the early emotional experiences of the child can give a particular orientation to his development as a man. But we cannot accept that the build-up of an objective world is to be solely attributed to a "sublimation" of drives. Together with Merleau-Ponty we look upon the body and its emotional equipment as "conditions of reason," they are "pre-values" of reason, they are implicitly rational. They constitute the first sources of giving meaning; they take care of the emotional or, as Werner expresses it,

---

52. Cf. *Les relations*, p. 10.

the "physiognomic" character of reality. By doing this, they present connecting links to reason when the latter makes its appearance as a positive power and calls forth new structures.

b. THE SECOND STEP: OBJECTIFICATION BY MEANS OF PRAXIS

The Necessity of Objectification

Objectification is not a kind of "original sin" of the human spirit. It is not an act of treason committed by a degenerate culture with respect to innocent nature, as was imagined by Rousseau, and it is not the work of a spirit that is the enemy of the soul, as Ludwig Klages has proclaimed.[53] Neither is it a "sublime melancholy of our lot," as Martin Buber believed.[54] But objectification is a step that must be taken on the way to becoming man. When we refer here to "becoming man," we are not primarily thinking of mankind's scientific and technical development, but of his social development, i.e., the Ego's becoming fully human with respect to a "you." When we reflect upon the matter, we clearly see that, to use again Buber's terms, we must speak the fundamental word "I-it" if the other fundamental word "I-you" is to be spoken with its full meaning.

The truth of this point manifests itself in the light of the preceding considerations. As we saw in Lecture Three, the "you" is believed, and "belief" is an affirmation of reality which is essentially independent of experience.[55] Let us now ask ourselves whether that description applies also to the above-mentioned attitude of a baby toward his mother. At first sight, one would be inclined to answer in the affirmative: of course, the infant believes in his mother. For he has not yet acquired any objectifying experiences; therefore, he is unable to compare his mother with any other reality. He cannot help believing in her. But it is precisely here that a doubt arises. Can one speak of "believing" when unbelief is not a real possibility? Isn't belief a free affirmation? Can one say of a faith that originates in a forced situation that it is a true faith?

An alternative to believing consent to the "you" as "you" does not arise for the child until he has begun to objectify. The child must first learn to know the totally other with respect to the "you." He must become estranged from the "you." This is, for the child, the way to become truly and fully an Ego. Before that, the child is but a non-autonomous part of a "we" and, by way of this "we," a part of a surrounding

---

53. *Der Geist als Wiedersacher der Seele,* 3 vols., 1929-32.
54. "Ich und Du," *Werke,* vol. I, p. 89.
55. Cf. above, p. 61.

world. Remplein speaks in this sense of a "symbiotic unity of child and world."[56]

Stone and Church express the same thought when they write: "Events or objects come into the baby's awareness in terms of immediate threat or gratification to him. Soon after, there may be a connection between things, but the connection is always personal, through the infant. Orange juice may signify that bath will follow, but these are related as things that happen to *him* in close succession, and not as events in a world. And there is the difficult part for most adults to grasp: although for the infant, everything is related to 'my' immediate needs, wants and experiences, there is no *me*. There simply is Hunger and Wetness, and Orange-Juice-Followed-by-Warm-Immersion, all in a context of familiar person and place; but there is no 'I am' hungry, or 'I feel' wet, or 'I taste' orange juice and so forth."[57]

Hence the famous Ego, considered to be the *a priori* center of every human awareness, does not necessarily exist. It does not exist as a thinking substance, nor as an "I think" that accompanies all acts of the mind, nor as an identical subject-pole, nor as a transcendental monad. It does not yet exist as a dialogal being that can be spoken to by a "you." It does not exist but it comes to be; and with respect to this coming-to-be we wish to draw attention here to some phenomena that are important for our purpose.

Practical Communication

How does the process of objectification and of the Ego's coming-to-be-aware of itself as Ego take place? Do the cognitive functions play a dominant role in that process? It is certain that, starting from the third month, the baby's senses are operating in a more refined way; for example, he has the ability to look with fixed attention at an object by adjusting his eyes. But for the Ego's coming-to-be it is "activity" and not "knowledge" that is of primary importance. From the "we-Ego" there arises in the first place the "action-Ego." The little child at that age is intent on moving and acting. He grasps, touches, handles and moves everything that is within his reach. But, as we have described earlier, his activities generally are forms of communication.[58] For instance, the child seizes a ring, but the ring, by its shape, lends itself to being grasped, it is a "cooperative object." The child opens and closes the cover of a box, but the cover, on its part, falls down with

---

56. *Entwicklung,* p. 222.
57. L.J. Stone and J. Church, *Children and Adolescence,* New York, 1957, p. 84. Hereafter abbreviated as *Childhood.*
58. See above, 66.

an interesting noise. The child shakes a rattle, but the rattle "reacts" with a funny sound.

This is even more true when the child begins to play. As F. Buyten-dijk has pointed out, man plays only with something that, on its part, plays with him.[59] When a little child plays with his toes, the fingers play with the toes and the toes with the fingers. The ball that bounces back in such a strange way is a fellow subject rather than an object. The child delights in throwing an object to the ground and thus rob-bing it of its "power." But the object is picked up and thus presents it-self once more as a cooperative play-object.[60] In this and many other similar ways the child experiences himself as the center of activity.

Everything that Werner has said about "things of action" applies to the objects here. "The preference for interpretation in terms of dynamic rather than static properties," he writes, "can be observed whenever the child is free to grasp the object in his own way."[61] What could be called a first constitution of space also arises in this way: "For the infant, surrounding space and private, corporally centered space are one, and together constitute an *Ur-raum*, i.e., 'primordial space'." And, appealing to the observations of William Stern, he continues: "The mouth is the primitive means of knowing objects, that is, in a literal sense, through the grasping of the objects. The spatial knowledge of an object results from a sucking in of the thing through the mouth. ... Out of this 'primordial space' there gradually arises ... a space-of-nearness, of propinquity, in which the space surrounding the body becomes differentiated from the body proper. Objects are known and orientated by reaching and touching, particularly with the hands."[62]

Similar remarks can be made with respect to the child's experience of time. Time also is constituted by actions and concrete processes that are important for the child. Werner gives the following examples: "A two-year old child says, for instance, 'Bath, bath!' and by these words expresses a desire in which the time element of the near future is in-volved by implication. The adverb of the future ('tomorrow,' 'soon,' etc.) is often identified with an immediate wish, just as the adverb of the past ('all done' etc.) is linked with satisfaction about some sort of completed activity."[63]

---

59. *Das Spiel von Mensch und Tier*, Berlin, 1933; "Het voetballen," *Tijd-schrift voor philosophie*, vol. 13 (1951), pp. 391-417.
60. Cf. F. Haigis, "Das Spiel als Begegnung," *Zeitschrift für Psychologie*, vol. 150 (1951), pp. 127 ff.
61. *Comparative ...* , pp. 68 f.
62. *Ibid., p.* 172 Cf. also *Childhood*, p. 88.
63. *Ibid.*, p. 185.

First Objectivity

Things lose their physiognomic character by being experimented with and manipulated. Remplein gives the following examples of this. Mother's fur-coat, which at first looked dangerous, appears to be perfectly safe after it has been examined by handling. A toddler who until now has anxiously avoided a red-hot stove later tries to act toward it as is done by adults.[64] In this way the little child realizes, at least for himself, a first degree of objectivity. The object is not yet for him the identical datum of different theoretical acts, but it is the identical "something" of varied practical activities. It goes without saying that such an objectivity is limited and unstable.

Stone and Church illustrate this point in the following way: "Although the baby becomes active with regard to objects, he still has to rely on the objects to tell him what to do. What they tell him depends on three things: 1. their action possibilities (stairs are to climb); 2. the baby's general readiness for action suggested by the object (stairs aren't anything at all if I am too young to climb them); and 3. his momentary state (stairs mean a lot more to me when I am not hungry; they are not very attractive when I've been on them ten times in a row)."[65]

Such a variable, limited objectivity that is related to the acting subject obviously cannot form the proper basis for a universal understanding. Yet, it is quite possible that acting subjects can to some extent understand one another on that basis. This is proved by developmental psychology. The child at that age seeks contact with other persons, imitates their movements, makes their facial expressions his own. Merleau-Ponty's theory of the body-subject, which we mentioned at the beginning, undoubtedly throws light on the intercommunication of subjects through practical behavior.

C. THE THIRD STEP: OBJECTIFICATION BY MEANS OF LANGUAGE

Specifically human behavior is characterized by the fact that it makes use of symbols. Here, too, we would be inclined to agree with Merleau-Ponty.[66] An action, gesture or sound can function as a symbol. However concrete a symbol may be, it is always something that takes the place of what is symbolized. In this sense we must say that the symbol is always to a certain degree abstract. Thus the formation of symbols is connected with human thinking. It is also generally accepted that speech is the most important of man's symbolizing

---

64. *Entwicklung*, p. 223.
65. *Childhood*, p. 88.
66. Cf. *La structure du comportement*, Paris, 4th ed., 1960, pp. 113 ff.

activities. This is so true that the best way of following the evolution of man's thought is a study of the development of his language.

Language, then, eminently is the means to constitute a relatively stable objective world. For the man who speaks uses a sound-symbol for a thing which he conceives as the identical bearer of definite activities, passivities, conditions and properties. This implies that the most important function of language for the constitution of a world is that of naming things.

Naming as Intentional Experience

This assertion also is obvious from developmental psychology. By giving names to things, the child definitively transcends the emotional relationship of the first phase and the purely practical relationship of the second phase. Let us illustrate this point by means of an example.

The sound "Mama" was for the little child first a cry of joy. Later "Mama" became the expression of a practical desire. It meant, for example, "I should like to be picked up." But finally "Mama" becomes the name of a person, albeit a person of particular importance for the child.[67] Now the word no longer has a purely expressive, or purely practical meaning for the child; it now has an intentional function. This means that the child's consciousness through and beyond the sound of "Mama" is directed to the person of his mother. As Remplein stresses, in agreement with Vincent Rüfner, " the novelty consists in knowledge about the meaning of a thing in 'intentional experience,' which also finds expression by pointing to the object."[68]

Typical of the child's new attitude is his desire to learn the names of things. He realizes that, thanks to the name, he can get a hold on reality. "The child is insatiable in demanding 'Whadda? whadda?', often without waiting for an answer," write Stone and Church. "It is almost as though the names had greater reality than the objects themselves, as though the objects took a new existence when fitted into the peculiarly human and intimate framework of language."[69]

At first, the child thinks of the grip he has on reality as a result of the name, as a magical influence. Hence his objectivity is not rational in nature. It can best be compared to the "objectivity of the everyday world," as we have characterized it elsewhere.[70] This, however, does

---

67. Cf. Remplein, *Entwicklung*, p. 203.
68. "Das Neuartige besteht im Wissen um die Bedeutung eines Dinges im 'intentionalen Erlebnis', das auch im Hindeuten auf den Gegenstand zum Ausdruck kommt." *Entwicklung*, p. 205. Cf. V. Rüfner, *Die Entfaltung des Seelischen*, Bamberg, 2nd ed., 1949, pp. 123-131.
69. *Childhood*, p. 120.
70. *Phenomenology and the Human Sciences*, pp. 88-97.

not remove the fact that naming is an intentional act of the child, an act that is directed to the surrounding world as well as to his own subjective conditions. "Just as names give shape and identity to the world, they also tell the toddler what is going on in himself and enable him to tell other people about it."[71]

The Phase of Protest and Its Dialogal Meaning

About three years of development finally make the child be what he ought to be according to classical phenomenology: he is now awareness of a world. The toddler considers himself a center of activities and experiences. As an Ego he directs himself intentionally to his objects; he learns to speak ever better about everything, about his world, his objects, his Ego. He speaks ever more logically and accurately. We might be inclined to say that now the harmony between that Ego and his "you," between the toddler and his mother, the three-year old and his parents, will be complete. What at first was only felt, what was experienced only anonymously, what was undergone only biologically, now can be expressed, communicated and shared with others. The dialogal relationship, one would suppose, now enters into a new, more perfect phase.

Undoubtedly it is true that the dialogal existence of the child enters into a new phase. But this phase is not at all idyllic. The development of the young awareness, as we have described it, changes into its dialectic opposite. The child who has learned to see himself as a center of activities and experiences also desires to look upon himself as an independent center. And what better way is there to show his autonomy than to direct his will against the will of the persons on whom he has been most dependent until now? This explains why the child now enters into a new phase of development that is characterized by unmanageability, willfulness and protest with respect to his parents.

According to Stone and Church, "Autonomy, in the sense both of the wish and the ability to be independent, appears as the salient trend of development during toddlerhood. ... As he becomes aware of his new abilities, he wants to exercise them for himself, without help or hindrance or coercion from other people. ... Perhaps the most striking display of the toddler's autonomy is his intermittent negativism, variously expressed by 'No!' "[72]

Spitz holds that this "no" plays a role even at an earlier time, in the form of a shaking of the head to express refusal and denial. He sees

---

71. *Childhood*, p. 120.
72. *Ibid.*, p. 112.

in this an important symbol that announces a new phase in libidinous relations.[73] Remplein looks upon the protest that turns up in the third year of the child as a "fundamental form of personal self-assertion."[74] All this indicates that what one would have expected to be the apex of the intimate mother-and-child dyad, a "world for us two," in reality ushers in a crisis. And this crisis puts an end to the exclusively or predominantly emotional dyad.

There is another contributive factor to that state of affairs. The language of the child, which at the beginning formed only the context of his concrete wishes, strivings and actions, now has the tendency to get away from such concrete things. It gradually acquires a more generalizing character; that is, the word becomes a symbol of a general concept. Let us illustrate this with an example. When a three-year old says, "Bow wow wow!" this means, "*This* dog barks." But later that same expression can have another meaning. The child then wants to say: "Don't you see, *dogs* bark."

It is true that this process of generalization goes on slowly. One may say that the six to ten year old child has at his disposal general concepts that are concerned at first with physical qualities and forms and later also with social and moral qualities.[75] According to Piaget, from the age of seven and eight, the magical way of looking at language begins to lose ground. Through his discussions with other people, the child gradually learns to distinguish between his subjective thinking and speaking, on the one hand, and the things that are signified, on the other.[76] This process fosters the development of a more objective, more realistic concept of the world.

Inevitably the child finally also assigns a place to his parents in his world that has become more realistic and more objective. The "you" becomes Mother, and later Mother becomes *a* mother, that is, *my* mother is *a* mother like other mothers, like the mothers of Johnny, Pete and Peggy. Here lies the beginning of the process of "becoming an other" (*Veränderung*) which has been philosophically clarified by Michael Theunissen.[77] As a consequence of this process the "you," which was unique in the original emotional dyad, becomes *the* other in reference to me through objectification, and finally one other among many similar others.

---

73. *Nein und Ja*, pp. 74-85.
74. *Entwicklung*, p. 244.
75. Cf. W. Neuhaus, *Der Aufbau der geistigen Welt des Kindes*, Munich, 1955.
76. *Le jugement et le raisonnement chez l'enfant*, 2nd ed., Neuchâtel, n.d., pp. 176, 191; *La représentation du monde chez l'enfant*, Paris, 3rd ed., 1947, p. 68.
77. *Der Andere*, pp. 85, ff.

Creation of Distance and Mediation as a Result of Language

What all this means is that language and thought now exist for themselves. They are the work of the human mind but also works that have their own laws and tendencies. Language enters as a medium between the Ego and the "you." It creates distance but also builds a bridge across this distance. While the feeling of early childhood is characterized by immediacy, by the absence of any distance, childhood speech is characterized by the fact that it creates distance but also mediates distances. For one who speaks is one who names everything from a distance and, at the same time, by speaking, he makes others share in the things he speaks of. The result is that one who speaks ultimately integrates everything and everyone into that great whole which is called, in the strict and proper sense, "*his* world." This constituting of a world is, as we have seen, characteristic of spiritual-material beings. There is truth in Hegel's saying that "the way of the mind is the detour."

The True Sense of the Reductions

The romanticist will be inclined to picture the feeling-of-becoming-one, the emotionally experienced dyad, as an ideal, but the philosopher cannot make such a view his own. For he knows that this emotional unity is something primitive, that it is based on elementary archetype experiences such as nearness, softness and warmth, and that it takes place, not in a world, but in a surrounding world.

The primitive dyadic idyll *must* therefore be disturbed. This, as we saw, is the dialogal meaning of the first phase of protest, of learning to speak and to think. The "no" and the conflicts and tensions resulting from it have, therefore, a positive function to fulfill. They make new forms of awareness possible, precisely because they make older forms of awareness impossible. New beings emerge, but only after the old beings that played a role in the toddler's consciousness have been stripped of their reality. New structures, for instance, causal relations, arise, but only at the cost of older structures, such as magical connections.

Such a "revolution" in human life we call a reduction. A reduction consists in this that a materially and formally determined world loses its reality. That world is devaluated, made relative, put between brackets. The decline of one world makes the emergence of a new world possible. And this change of appearance of that-which-is-for-me is the positive meaning of reduction.

Something like this takes place in the life of man but it is not a "deed" of man himself. The reduction — as we see it — is not a thought experiment, not an act of the will, not a spontaneous change of attitude. It is true that no reduction is conceivable without me, but the complementary thesis is equally true, viz., that no reduction is exclusively *my* work. It is something that comes over me and that I accept; it is a "destiny."

The reason is that the reduction of the old world and the birth of the new world flow from my dialogue with a "you," with the other, with others. Word and repartee are spoken in freedom but also with necessity. I do something in this dialogue but I also undergo something; I give and receive, I change and am changed. The one is inconceivable without the other, if it is true, as we have stated at the beginning, that the dialogal event is the expression of reciprocity.[78]

The breaking up of the primitive dyad is a revolution in the life of the child, a revolution that does not occur without violence. There is hesitation, uncertainty, confusion; there is conflict in the child and conflict between the child and others. There is protest, opposition, refusal. But, once again, this conflict is necessary if the dialogue is to enter a new phase, if new dimensions of the child's existence are to become involved in the "discourse." If this does not take place, the dialogue remains frozen at a particular level of experience, thought and speech. It then degenerates into "idle talk" (*Gerede*).

Reflection

We have not yet finished our description of the awakening and development of awareness in a young child, for we have not yet spoken of reflection. The power and inclination to reflect awaken only in adolescence. At this stage the young person views himself as an interiority that is unique and that, therefore, differs and is separated from the interiority of other persons. Only then, as Merleau-Ponty points out, is there question of a *cogito*.[79] According to Remplein, the child thought of himself as a practical Ego, but when he reaches puberty "man turns his gaze inwards and finds in himself a world of thoughts, feelings, dispositions, passions, inclinations, tendencies and desires; he discovers his inner self."[80]

P. J. Calon notes that "it is usually only after the fifteenth year that what is really one's own, what belong to the interior life, expands more fully."[81] Eduard Spranger does not hesitate to speak of a "discovery of

---

78. Cf. above, pp. 64 f.
79. *Phénoménologie de la perception*, p. 408.
80. In adolescene "wendet der Mensch seinen Blick nach innen und findet in sich die Welt der Gedanken, Gefühle, Stimmungen, Affekte, Triebe, Strebungen und Begierden, er entdeckt sein *seelisches Ich.*" *Entwicklung*, p. 428.
81. *De jongen. De psychologie van de jongen van de laatste schooljaren tot aan de volwassen leeftijd*, Heemstede, 1953.

the subject as of a world for himself that is always separated like an island from everything else in the world, from things and men — a discovery which on that account is the experience of great loneliness."[82]

Stone and Church use a less philosophical language, but they express essentially the same thought in their characterization of adolescence: "The central theme of adolescene is the finding of one's self. . . . This means an intensified self-awareness — largely manifested as *self-consciousness* — and a new push for independence. . . . The older adolescent . . . must now find an identity as himself rather than as a member either of his family or his gang."[83] Thus these young people in our Western culture who have reached adolescence actually experience to some extent what Descartes, Husserl and Sartre have thought. It is also well known that the above-described reduction of the child's realistic world and the reflective discovery of his own subjective interiority by the adolescent are, in their turn, accompanied by doubts, crises and conflicts. But we cannot enter into this problem here.

3. Conclusions

We have now sufficiently examined the coming-to-be of awareness to draw some important conclusions. These can be briefly summarized as follows.

Awareness as an Ego's mode of being has no static character, but is constantly subject to change. The changes concern the "what" as well as the "how," the content as well as the structures. If we call the actual and possible beings that are real for an aware Ego its "world," we must admit also that this world is changeable from the material and the formal standpoint. Because the Ego exists "in" its world, a radical change of this world results in a crisis of the Ego's existence.

Now, being-aware of a world that is composed of actual and possible intentional objects is, genetically speaking, a relatively late form of awareness. It arises at the same time as the development of language and the more generalizing use of languge symbols. The reflective discovery of the so-called "inner world" occurs even later; it only comes about at the time of adolescence. Two other modes of becoming aware precede the objectifying and reflective forms of awareness — namely, the emotional-biological mode and the practical-objectifying mode.

Our knowledge of the other as an Ego is rooted in the most original,

---

82. " . . . Entdeckung des Subjekts als einer Welt für sich, die auf immer inselhaft getrennt ist von allem andern in der Welt, Dingen und Menschen — und damit das Erlebnis der groszen Einsamkeit." *Psychologie des Jugendalters,* Heidelberg, 23rd ed., 1953, pp. 34 f.

83. *Childhood,* p. 270.

the non-objectifying mode of awareness. For that upon which a subject is first emotionally and biologically dependent is his fellow subject. We have characterized the mode in which the presence of a fellow subject is primarily experienced by using the formula: the feeling subject feels himself by the fact that he feels his fellow subject.

It is now no longer difficult to see what turn is taken by the further development of being-aware. What was originally a unity — feeling oneself and feeling the other — is split. The subject who feels himself as a fellow subject realizes that he is an autonomous Ego which feels a non-Ego that exists independently of him. In this way the fellow subject changes into a non-Ego and into an object. The subject who feels himself becomes, in turn, an Ego which through thought reflects upon itself. He reflects upon his own Ego, independently of the existence of a non-Ego. This results in the well-known division of experience into "sensation" and "reflection," and of the world into an "outer world" and an "inner world." Philosophers like Descartes and others who are influenced by him look upon that division as an original and necessary datum.

The objectifying and reflective awareness, however, is, as we have shown, only an "upper layer" even in adults. It is true that our original feeling and emotional mode of being-aware is hidden by it, but it continues to exist. It manifests itself when a situation appears to an Ego in such a way that this Ego is unable to keep itself at a distance from it (emotion), or when, from the start, there is no distance (feeling). There is no distance when I am present to the other in an intimate way. This most elementary of all human situations — we together in a surrounding world — is not primarily experienced, thought or striven for, but is first of all lived in a feeling way. This makes it understandable how we can be present to the other in a wholly "natural" way; on the other hand, it is evident that a philosophy of immanence, reflection and intentionality cannot explain that presence.

LECTURE FIVE
THE GROWTH OF FREEDOM

1. Freedom and Its Meaning

Are There Proofs for the Existence of Freedom?

Freedom is one of the important topics of phenomenological thinking. It stands at the center of existential philosophy and much attention is given to it by existential phenomenology. What is typical of the way the representatives of these philosophies deal with this topic is the fact that they make no attempt to prove that man is free. Unlike many nineteenth century authors, they feel that such an endeavor would be useless; they know that freedom is more fundamental than are the results of reasoning and arguing. For it is precisely freedom that makes possible man's efforts to show something, to bring something to light, to express something meaningful.

The phenomenologist, then, is inclined to put human freedom among the fundamental data that cannot be proved and do not need to be proved. For the absolute denial of freedom — which is called determinism — leads to absurd consequences. As Alphonse De Waelhens rightly remarks, "If it belongs to the human condition to discover and establish meanings, the idea that determinism could apply to man simply becomes absurd."[1]

It would be possible to apply the phenomenological theory of evidence to freedom. One could then start from the actual situation of the philosopher and ask, What does he actually do? He expounds ideas; he speaks to others; he writes for others. In every case he conducts a dialogue with actual or possible fellow philosophers. Thus he tacitly assumes that the others possess the power to accept or reject his arguments. He judges that the others can agree or disagree, can say yes or no. This shows that the philosopher in the concrete pursuit of his task presupposes the freedom of those to whom he addresses himself, regardless of the philosophical school, trend or opinion which he espouses. Even if he is a naturalist, a materialist or a positivist, he does not have discussions with mechanical contraptions, robots or cybernetic machines.

---

1. " . . . si la condition de l'homme est de découvrir et établir des significations, l'idée que le déterminisme pourrait s'appliquer à l'homme devient simplement absurde." "Linéaments d'une interprétation phénoménologique de la liberté," *Actes du 4e congrès des sociétés de philosophie de langue française,* Neuchâtel, 1949, p. 83.

A general and necessary difference manifests itself here. Machines, however ingeniously constructed, are things we use; men, on the contrary, we try to persuade, that is, we invite them to agree with our views, but we do not force them. We desire that they respond with a spontaneous agreement. And, once more, in this there is a tacit acknowledgment of the fact that our human partners are free.

The Apodictic Character of Freedom

The phenomenologist will perhaps even go further and refer to human freedom as apodictically evident. According to Husserl, an apodictic evidence is characterized by the fact that a critical reflection discloses that the non-existence of the evident state of affairs is something inconceivable.[2] Now, anyone who critically reflects upon the existence of freedom by that very fact affirms what he had attempted to deny. His antithesis does not relativize the thesis of the existence of human freedom, it does not limit it or attack its validity, but confirms it. The thesis is absolutely valid because the antithesis is not tenable. The thesis is apodictically evident in the Husserlian sense.

At this point, however, begins a confusion of ideas introduced by existential philosophy. The thesis concerning the existence of human freedom is absolutely valid; of this we should be convinced. But does this mean that human freedom is an absolute freedom? Obviously, such a conclusion cannot be justified on logical grounds. A thesis that is absolutely valid is not the same as a thesis whose content is absolute. But, one may ask, is it possible to show the absolute character of human freedom in a phenomenological way? This is a question that deserves to be examined.

Absolute Freedom

Let us start with the dialogue which, in fact, we are always engaged in — for instance, by writing these lines or reading them — and ask ourselves the question: Is such a dialogue conceivable if we, the writers or readers, the speakers or listeners, are absolutely free beings? The meaning of this critical question is, of course, intimately connected with the content of the concepts "free" and "absolutely free." We will not be able to answer that question unless we first define those concepts at least to a certain extent. Let us, therefore, provisionally define freedom with Karl Jaspers as "the choice of my Self"[3] and speak of absolute freedom when I, and no one else, is the subject who makes the choice. In other words, I am the origin, without any qualification,

---

2. *Cart. Medit.*, p. 56.
3. *Philosophie*, Vol. II, *Existenzerhellung*, Berlin, 1932, p. 182.

of my deeds, my decisions, my actions, in short, of my whole being. Let us emphasize it again, this means that I myself, and no one else or nothing else, am that source or origin.

Three Laws of the True Dialogue

It stands to reason that a dialogue is conceivable only when I let the other see what I see, and when something that is meaningful for the other can, in principle, also become meaningful for me. This fact is important in two respects. It shows, first of all, that a dialogue requires at least three beings, viz., two who speak with each other and whom we look upon as the "subjects" of the dialogue, and something about which they speak. This something one can hardly avoid calling the "object" of their discourse. Even when the two partners in a dialogue converse about themselves, there is "something" that engages their attention, something to which they are intentionally related, and this "something" is their "object."

We may, therefore, repeat here a point stressed in the preceding lecture, namely, that objectification should never be looked upon as a degenerating procedure; on the contrary, the object is present in the human dialogue from the very beginning.

Something else, however, also becomes evident. Each of the two partners in the dialogue must adjust himself to something which he himself is not; this he must do in a threefold respect:

1. He must adjust himself to his partner in the dialogue by listening and answering, by affirming and denying, by doubting and agreeing.

2. He must take a stand in relation to the "something" that is the object of the dialogue. For example, he perceives the object or imagines it, determines its value, characterizes it as good or bad, useful or harmful, true or false, beautiful or ugly. All this demands objectifying intentions that culminate in a certain judgment, a conclusion stating that it is so and not otherwise. And these intentions are, of course, objectifying only if they take into account the proper character of the object. For example, no matter how free a subject may be, he cannot claim that a judgment is green in color or that the color green is immoral. The proper character of the object — the judgment or the color — does not permit such a statement.

3. The subject who is engaged in a dialogue must relate himself to the object under discussion in such a way that an understanding and agreement with his interlocutor is not *a priori* excluded. Let us explain this point by means of an example. Suppose that I discuss the artistic value of a play with a friend. At first, we are not in agreement. In order to reach an agreement, we then analyze and critically examine the under-

lying plot, the action, the characterization of the actors, the dramatic structure and the dialogue of the play. Both of us then apply all kinds of aesthetic standards to the object under discussion. In this way, in spite of our original disagreement, it is in principle possible that we will reach the same judgment and evaluation of the play.

Let us suppose now that my interlocutor considers the value of the play solely from the standpoint of the financial gains to be attained by its performance; in other words, he uses only economic categories whereas I think in terms of artistic values. In such a case no actual agreement is possible between us. The reason is that we approach the object in different ways. Each one bases his knowing and evaluating mind on the matter under consideration, but in manners that are formally diverse. In such circumstances the dialogue in question is only a pseudo-dialogue, only a juxtaposition of two monologues.

If we reserve the term "dialogue" in its authentic sense to a communication between two persons which, in principle, can lead to an agreement between them, then, as the preceding brief analysis shows, every authentic dialogue obeys three laws:

1. In speaking and listening I must adjust myself to the "you" with whom I hold a dialogue. This law flows from the principle of reciprocity.[4]

2. In knowing, evaluating and striving I must adjust myself to the matter that happens to be the object of our dialogue.

3. In knowing, evaluating and striving I must approach the matter under discussion in a way that is formally the same as that of the "you" with whom I am in dialogue.

Dialogue and Absolute Freedom

If our analysis is sound, it shows that the one who engages in a dialogue cannot be free in the sbsolute sense described above. For the source of his speaking and listening is not himself as an isolated individual, but it is himself in relation to the other. Moreover, the objectivity of his speech is not guaranteed by himself alone but by his subordination to the object in question. For, as we saw, the speaker must adjust himself to his object. It is not enough, however, that he adapt himself to the object; he must also adjust himself to the object in a definite way, a particular style; and in the choice of this style he must take into account the choice made by the other person with whom he seeks to reach an agreement.

From this we conclude that the freedom of one who is engaged in a

---

4. Cf. above, pp. 64 f.

dialogue is limited in a threefold way: by the other's freedom, by the mode of being of the object under discussion, and by the way he must speak to the other about the object.

These conclusions do not merely have a theoretical importance; practical decisions also are made on the basis of the agreement or disagreement with the others. As a matter of fact, this is what usually happens in man's social life. Great decisions in personal, economic, religious or political matters are not arrived at without testing them by comparing them with the views of others.

It is possible, of course, for a reformer, a genius or a revolutionary to reach a conviction that departs from the convictions of everyone else in his surroundings. But the reformer's or revolutionary's rejection of the accepted views also is conceivable only after he has acquired knowledge of those views. His opposition is inconceivable without the others whose theory or practice he opposes. The revolutionary, then, cannot consider himself as the exclusive source of his decisions and actions. The others have, from the very beginning, contributed to the formation of his view, albeit in a negative way.

Let us now ask ourselves what absolute freedom, in the above-described sense, would mean. Such a freedom is evidently conceivable only as absolute autonomy, inviolable sovereignty, total autarky. For only then would the free person himself be the exclusive origin of his deeds, his decisions, his being. But concepts such as "autonomy" and "autarky" really have played a role in the history of human thought.

We will see more about that later. Here we will limit ourselves to establishing the fact that a dialogue between absolutely free beings is an impossibility. Neither theoretically nor practically could such beings communicate with one another; they could not exist as social beings. Merleau-Ponty's claim that human life has, from its very beginning, a social dimension[5] is a claim that we should accept, and this claim cannot possibly be reconciled with the postulates of certain existential philosophers, who make man an absolutely free being. But social life, communication and dialogue between absolutely free beings is as impossible as is social life, communication and dialogue between cybernetic machines.

This is not a new discovery. As early as 1831 Johann Friedrich Herbart came to the conclusion that a philosophy of education can be based neither upon a materialistic foundation nor upon a transcendental-idealistic foundation. "Philosophical systems," he wrote, "which accept either *fatalism* or *transcendental freedom* automatical-

---

5. *Phénoménologie de la perception*, p. 448.

ly exclude pedagogy."[6] The scope of Herbart's remark is in no way confined to the field of education. As Herbert Hornstein observes,[7] Herbart's problem applies to the possibility of communication in general and — we may add here — the possibility of interhuman relationships and social life in general. A phenomenology that does not from the very beginning take those original data into account, is defective. But the question that must still be asked is, What philosophical conclusions must be drawn from our critique of absolute freedom?

2. How Is Finite Freedom Possible?

One thing, at least, has become evident: the dilemma "either free will or determinism," which was the object of so many violent debates in the past, is not very meaningful. There is a temptation to go from the rejection of determinism to the acceptance of indeterminism or absolute freedom. In reality, however, the thesis of absolute freedom is as untenable as that of absolute unfreedom.

The solution of our problem, then, seems to be obvious. Only the idea of a finite freedom, one could say, can be applied to humanity as it really is. The historical, social, economical and political life of mankind manifests over and over again a limited freedom. And the examination of the lives of individuals also reveals that human freedom has its limits.

Unfortunately, things are not that simple. Any seasoned philosopher knows how difficult it is to justify the concept of a finite freedom. It is not easy to refute the objections of the idealists, particularly the transcendental idealist. By what, he will ask, is my freedom restricted. By something that is not free? But the non-free is essentially an object for one who is free; hence it cannot limit freedom. Can my freedom, then, be restricted by the freedom of someone else? This, too, will be contested by the transcendental idealist. The other's freedom, he will say, has a certain validity for me, that is, it is known, understood and constituted as freedom by me. In other words, it is an intentional object for me. But my knowledge of this being-free, my constitution of this object "freedom," simply means an enlargement of my own freedom. And the idealist's conclusion is: my freedom is limitless. There is no such thing as more or less freedom. Freedom is absolute or not at all.

This, in a very general way, is what the transcendental idealist thinks. But if we wish to understand what philosophers have actually maintained, it will be necessary to go into the history of thought. Let

6. *Umrisz pädagogischer Vorlesungen*, par. 3.
7. *Bildsamkeit und Freiheit*, Düsseldorf, 1959.

us, then, briefly survey here the philosophical development that led
to the birth of the above-mentioned idea of absolute freedom.

Historical Survey

The idea of the individual man's unconditional freedom was entirely unknown in Antiquity. According to Greek and Roman thinking, the free citizen exercised his rights in conformity with the laws of
the *polis*, the gods, the *cosmos* and the *logos*. Neither were the Christian
Middle Ages familiar with the problem of absolute freedom. According to the Scholastic philosophers, man could act with freedom within the framework of his nature. Man's nature owed its reality to the
creative thought of God; this nature was the measure and, at the
same time, the unsurpassable limit of free human action.

It is only in Descartes that we find an idea pointing toward a concept of absolute freedom. According to the Cartesian view, the human
soul is spirit, consciousness and self-consciousness, and nothing else.
The spiritual soul has also the power to will freely; and in this respect
it is not essentially different from the divine act of willing.[8]

Kant goes even further by introducing the idea of autonomy. "Autonomy," according to Kant, is "the property of the will to be a law to
itself, independently of all properties of the objects of willing."[9] While
it is true that he who acts morally obeys an unconditional imperative,
he hears the voice of this imperative exclusively in himself.

The dialectic of Hegel demands the limitlessness of spiritual knowing and hence, at the same time the limitlessness of spiritual freedom. "Only the ignorant is limited, for he has no knowledge of any
limits," says Hegel. "On the contrary, he who knows about limits,
knows about them . . . as something known. . . . Hence to know about
one's limits means to know about one's limitlessness."[10] According to
Hegel, the knowing, evaluating, actively self-developing life of the
Spirit is exclusively related to itself. It includes all contradictions in
itself. Hence the freedom of the Spirit is unlimited. It is the freedom
of everyone and of everything. For that reason it is at the same time

---

8. *Meditationes de prima philosophia*, IV Med., Pléiade ed., Paris, 1952, p.
305.

9. " . . . die Beschaffenheit des Willens, dadurch derselbe ihm selbst (unab-
hängig von aller Beschaffenheit der Gegenstände des Wollens) ein Gesetz ist."
Grundlegung zur Metaphysik der Sitten, Reklam ed., p. 95.

10. "Nur der Unwissende ist beschränkt, denn er weisz von keiner Schranke.
Wer dagegen von der Schranke weisz, der weisz von ihr . . . als von einem Ge-
wuszten . . . Von seiner Schranke wissen heiszt daher, von seiner Unbeschränkt-
heit wissen." *Werke*, Jubiläumausgabe, vol. X, p. 44.

the freedom of no one and of nothing, but a mere "phantom" (Jaspers).[11]

Max Stirner, a Left Wing Hegelian, drew a radical conclusion from Hegel's viewpoint. He replaced the unique freedom of the phantom-Ego by the unique freedom of his own concrete Ego. The freedom of the Spirit assumes in Stirner the form of creative individuality. "Ownness," individuality, "created a new freedom," he says, "for ownness is the creator of all."[12]

The modern ethos of individual freedom attains its sharpest expression in the existentialistic philosophy of Jean-Paul Sartre. According to Sartre, the individual man calls his own essence into existence, and he does this by the fact that he is a free self-project. Because God is dead, human existence exercises the rights which is the Middle Ages were reserved for God's thinking: man becomes the creator of his own essence.[13] Man's freedom consists in this that he realizes himself by existing. In this he, ultimately, does not let himself be motivated by anything or anyone. Sartre glorifies the arbitrariness of free choice, the "gratuitousness of choice."[14] Neither motives nor laws of logic are able to impose rules on the man who is a free self-project. "Choose," Sartre exclaims, "that is, invent."[15] One's past, too, presents no obligatory character with respect to existence.

Sartre maintains that every free action is a "nihilation," a divorcing oneself from the Ego one has been. All this applies not only to the individual, for, by choosing himself, man, at the same time, chooses his fellowmen and is responsible for the whole of mankind.[16] This self-justifying freedom constitutes, according to some existential philosophers, the authentic being of man. Man simply "is" freedom to choose, and he "is" by choosing.

Pseudo-infinity

This brief survey enables us to characterize to some extent the course of the philosophical development that has culminated in modern absolutism with respect to freedom. In spite of the great differences existing between the thinkers, the schools and trends of thought we have

---

11. *Existenzerhellung,* pp. 192, 194.
12. "Die Eigenheit erschuf eine neue Freiheit, denn die Eigenheit ist Schöpferin von Allem." *Der Einzige und sein Eigentum,* Reklam, n.d., Leipzig, p. 192.
13. *L'existentialisme est un humanisme,* Paris, 1954, pp. 22 ff.
13a. *Die Krise . . . ,* pp. 335, 336.
14. *L'être et le néant,* pp. 513, 519.
15. *L'existentialisme est un humanisme,* p. 47.
16. *Ibid.,* pp. 25-27. It is true that in *L'être et le néant* Sartre developed a different philosophy of the other Ego. According to this work, the only possible relationship between an Ego and another Ego is that of reciprocal "nihilation."

briefly surveyed, we discover also a certain agreement among them in the "style" of their thinking. The development that began with Descartes' *cogito, sum* (I think, I am), ends with the passionate *eligendo sum* (I am by choosing) of existentialist philosophers.

When we ask what these diverse views have in common, we must answer that all of them are characterized by a self-reflective way of thinking. The philosophers we have mentioned start from a consciousness that is concerned with itself, a self-determining morality, a Spirit that develops by self-evoked contradictions, an existence striving for self-realization. So the question which imposes itself here is whether this point is not "the original falsehood" that has led to the puzzling development surveyed above.

We look upon the one-sided self-reflective way of thinking as something dangerous because it calls forth the mistaken illusion of infinity. It is true, of course, that I can reflect upon myself in an endless way. There arises an endless circuit between myself as reflecting and myself as the one I reflect upon — which makes Sartre speak of a "circuit of ipseity."[17] This endless circuit makes us forget that I, while thus reflecting, remain encapsulated within myself. There arises a pseudo-infinity because the decisive dimension is absent, viz., the dimension that makes possible a real turning-toward and a real turning-away-from. As early as 1922 Martin Buber warned against what he called the "monologal fundamental movement of the mind." This movement, as he expressed it, is "not a turning-away-from in contrast with a turning-to, but is a bending-backwards" of the mind on itself.[18]

Conflict and Agreement

The introduction of pseudo-infinity into philosophical discussions leads to absurd consequences. One of these we will discuss here, namely, the uniqueness of the freedom that is exclusively related to itself.

Anyone who has sufficiently reflected upon the problem realizes that a freedom whose development includes all freedoms, or a freedom that co-constitutes all other freedoms by the fact of constituting itself, or a freedom that chooses all other freedoms by choosing itself, is a unique freedom. By this expression we mean that its existence excludes the existence of other independent freedoms.

The idea of communication, speech or dialogue is, of course, in contradiction with the postulate of such an absolute and unique freedom.

---

17. *L'être et le néant,* pp. 147 ff.
18. "... nicht Abwendung im Gegensatz, sondern Rückbiegung." "Zwiesprache," *Das dialogische Prinzip,* Heidelberg, 1962, p. 171.

For, we repeat, the postulate of uniqueness cannot be reconciled with the idea of turning-to and turning-away-from. To this we must add that such a way of thinking leaves no room either for genuine agreement or for genuine conflict.

What do we mean by a "genuine conflict"? A conflict is genuine when it can, in principle, lead to the elimination of one of the existences that are involved in the struggle. An agreement is genuine when a genuine conflict is possible. These two assertions obviously are interconnected. For peace, concord and harmony between free existences are valuable precisely because murder, war and the destruction of free existences are concrete possibilities. No philosopher who wants to formulate an ethical, social or political philosophy can completely disregard that fact.

But it is typical of the representatives of monologal philosophy that they shrink away from that consequence. Even Hegel and Sartre, the two leading philosophers of conflict, do not want to have anything to do with the "annihilation" of a finite and free consciousness.

In Hegel's famous chapter on the Master and the Slave there is a "life and death struggle" between the two consciousnesses, but this battle ends with the subjection of the Slave and not with his death.[19] Sartre, in his main work, BEING AND NOTHINGNESS, often speaks of "nihilation" but not of "annihilation." Sartre realizes that the hatred of a conscious being tends to the annihilation of another conscious being. But, he tells us, the other who could be annihilated by the hater would continue to live for the latter's consciousness as one who has had existence. Hence his annihilation would be useless.[20]

Sartre assumes here — as he always does in his phenomenological ontology — that every consciousness projects its own world. On that account he comes to conclusions that impress us as unreal. From the phenomenological standpoint we must affirm that the other is not hated as a pure consciousness but as somebody who, together with me, lives in a common surrounding world and who by his existence and activity gives a particular character to that world. If the other is annihilated, his existence and activity cease. The surrounding world then takes on the character which *I* give to it.

The reason why both Hegel and Sartre evade the problem of the conflict-unto-the-finish is simple. A conflict with a lethal finish presupposes the mutually independent existence of several conscious free beings that communicate with one another. But this is something

---

19. *Phänomenologie des Geistes,* pp. 123-131.
20. *L'être et le néant,* p. 483.

which neither Hegel nor Sartre can accept within the framework of their respective systems.

Man as an "Animal to Be Freed"

All this shows that modern thinking about human freedom has more or less come to an impasse. If we wish to help set it into motion once more, we will have to get rid of inveterate and deeply rooted habits of thought.

The first prejudice we must get rid of is the conviction that freedom, in the sense of the individual's fully developed ability to dispose of himself, is an ontological characteristic of man. From a historical standpoint this conviction is very debatable. As Georg Gusdorf extensively proves in his valuable work about the human meaning of freedom,[21] the typically Western concept of individual freedom, sketched above, is the end result of a religious, philosophical and political development which has been going on for about one thousand years.

Moreover, even some existential philosophers have pointed out that every individual man must free himself, must appropriate freedom as his own possibility. In a negative way this means that he does not willy-nilly become free, that freedom is not conferred upon him, as it were, from without. This is a valuable thought, but it needs to be freed from the straightjacket of existential-philosophical individualism.

Perhaps the problem of free activity is the same as that of other specifically human ways of acting. With respect to typically human abilities Helmuth Plessner points out that "man's idea of himself as man lifts the gifts of speaking, acting, shaping, laughing and crying ... from the totality of human capacities; it draws them forth from that totality, it is the first condition of those gifts, their principle of organization and delimitation, and takes care that they remain gifts that can be cultivated."[22] Aren't these words applicable also to the gift of free activity? Do they not contain a directive concerning the way by which we can escape from the unfruitful circle of monologal thinking?

Two things are important in relation to our problem. First, man's idea of himself as a free being is decisive for the concrete pursuit of freedom by different peoples and in different historical periods; other-

---

21. *Signification humaine de la liberté,* Paris, 1962.
22. "Die Auffassung des Menschen von sich als Menschen hebt die Gaben des Sprechens, Handelns, Gestaltens, Lachens und Weinens ... aus der Fülle menschlicher Fähigkeit heraus, entlockt sie ihr, ist ihre erste Bedingung, Prinzip ihrer Gliederung und Abgrenzung und sorgt dafür, dasz sie kultivierbare Gaben bleiben." *Lachen und Weinen,* Bern, 2nd ed., 1950, p. 11.

wise the evolution of the idea of freedom, described by Gusdorf, would be inexplicable. Secondly, it is evident that man's idea of what it means to be free is always older than the *individual* man. This idea obviously lives in a *society* of free men. Thus it presupposes not only social life in general but also this or that concrete form of social life.

From this we may conclude that the individual man can become free only if he is born in a society of free men and is brought up within the framework of such society. This assertion, however, does not deny the existence of a specific human nature. It belongs to man's nature, we can say, that he has the capacity to appropriate freedom when it is offered to him; and this is a capacity which a machine or an animal do not have. This capacity undoubtedly is an important characteristic of man's nature.

3. Conclusions

The Importance of the Genetic and Social View

The methodical conclusion to be drawn from all this is that it is necessary to complement the historical view of freedom with genetic and social considerations. Both of these must become the object of a proper philosophical reflection. The phenomenon of change from generation to generation must become the theme of philosophical anthropology. Here, however, we can develop only a few of the fundamental ideas. To illustrate what we have in mind, let us compare our view to a completely different conception.

The German poet Friedriech Schiller, who was influenced by Kant, wrote in one of his works: "Man is created free, and free he is even though he is born in chains." These words express a metaphysical, moral and religious postulate, but they do not agree with experience. From the phenomenological standpoint we must say that man when, where and in whatever circumstances he is born, is not free. When he is born he is as much governed by biological needs and drives as is a young animal. We also know that man still appears as an animal if, after his birth, he grows up among animals. This is proved by the experiences gathered in the eighteenth century with the "Savage of Aveyron" and in our century with the "wolf-children of Midnapore."[23]

All this shows and confirms our fundamental idea that man at birth appears as an "animal to be freed." This means that it is the free adults who make freedom germinate in the child who is not yet free. This

---

23. Cf. Jean E. Itard, *De l'éducation d'un homme sauvage*, 1801; *Die Wolfskinder von Midnapore*, mit einem Geleitwort von Adolf Portmann, Heidelberg, 1964.

liberation requires that the child discover the possibility of freedom
as *his* possibility, just as he must also actively appropriate to himself
the possibility of speech, morality and culture. But the child can make
the gift of freedom his own only by spontaneously turning to the others, the adults. The turning to the others, therefore, is the first step
on the road to self-liberation.

Accordingly, Sartre is right when he says that man, by choosing
himself, chooses the others. But this is only half the truth. The complementary truth is that man is not able to choose himself unless he
is first chosen by others. Only through this does a free relationship
arise. For relation is, according to Buber, "at the same time to be
chosen and to choose, 'passion' and action."[24]

Finite Freedom

From this we can conclude that man does not at first possess absolute freedom and then later autonomously decide whether he will or
will not enter into relations with others. Such an absolute freedom
does not agree with reality. On the contrary, relationship stands at the
cradle of human freedom, and this relationship is a factual one; it
corresponds to a facticity.

We have thus replied to the question how a finite freedom is possible. Human freedom does not become finite either through external
limitations or through self-limitation. It is finite because it springs
from a relationship; it is finite because, as choosing, it is chosen; it is
finite because that choice was a factical choice.

Freedom and Arbitrariness

The destiny of a freedom resulting from a relationship is to enter
into relationship. If it refuses to obey its destiny, if it does not want to
relate with others, it degenerates into arbitrariness. A choice as such
is not arbitrary, but arbitrariness belongs only to a choice resulting
from the chooser's turning to himself as the sovereign subject of the
decision.

Let us clarify this point by recalling a classical example of arbitrariness. Consider the case of a Roman emperor, who watches the
gladiators' combat in the arena and decides with a motion of his hand
whether the loser should be killed or spared. The emperor is not in the
least concerned for the loser as a person. The gladiator is a slave kept
alive solely in order to risk his life. There is no motive that can be
shown for either killing him or sparing his life. And precisely because
there are no motives, the decision is solely based on the individual

---

24. *Das dialogische Prinzip,* p. 15.

subjectivity of the emperor. He is aware of the fact that it depends on his pleasure alone whether the loser will live or die. In other words, the emperor reflects exclusively upon himself, his power, his sovereignty, his right to make a decision for which he does not have to render an account to anyone.

This brief analysis shows that arbitrariness is the exercise of freedom without turning to others. If, on the contrary, the free agent enters into relationship with others, it is still possible for him to make a mistake, to come to a wrong conclusion, or to act unjustly, but he will not have acted in an arbitrary way.

Arbitrariness comes about when an acting Ego reflects exclusively upon its own freedom; arbitrariness flows from the intoxicating consciousness of pseudo-infinity. But one who is conscious of his responsibility toward others knows the limit of his freedom. For the limit of his freedom is the freedom of the other.

Yet, this expression is not entirely correct. In the sense of our preceding analyses,[25] we should say that the other's freedom does not *primarily* appear to me as a clearly discernible limit. It is true, of course, that people, through conventional stipulations, moral precepts, laws and political agreements, have drawn *secondary* limits. These serve to distinguish the moral and legal pursuit of freedom from its immoral and illegal pursuit. The question of what those rules should contain, of where the limits should be drawn, is answered differently by different peoples; moreover, their views change in the course of history. It should be evident, however, that conventional, moral, legal and political rules can be formulated only because of the fact that every man vaguely realizes the finite nature of his freedom. I have an original awareness of the other's freedom and of the fact that I must respect this freedom "somewhere." For this reason the other's freedom can be compared to a horizon rather than a limit.

It is true that modern sciences, such as psychology, psychiatry, sociology, anthropology and economics, have constructed typologies, theories and models of the pursuit of human freedom. These theories and models are useful and even indispensable, as we have stressed elsewhere.[26] Let us repeat it once more, objectification and the resulting formalization are not to be looked upon as "sins against the Holy Spirit." It is impossible to organize modern society in a meaningful way without applying the methods developed within the framework of the human sciences. But those who pursue those sciences should not forget that their models of *probable* pursuit of freedom

---

25. Cf. above, pp. 29 ff.
26. *Phenomenology and the Human Sciences,* Pittsburgh, 1963.

are by their very nature only *approximations*. They are more or less imperfect, since precisely in the field of human freedom the most unlikely things can happen. The other's freedom is ultimately the other's mystery; and precisely because I can never predict with perfect certainty how the other will act in freedom, my freedom with respect to him is limited.

LECTURE SIX

THE GROWTH OF FAITH

1. Introduction: The Question About the "You"

My finite freedom is destined, we saw, to enter into relationship; I am called to encounter a "you." And because this destiny determines my life from the start, the "you" for whom I am destined and by whom I feel called must be older than me. This is the fundamental idea that we intend to develop in this lecture. But before we can do this, certain areas of confusion must first be discussed. The obvious question to arise is, of course, "Who is that 'you' that is constantly referred to?"

This question is wholly reasonable — and all the more so because we seem to waver in our speaking about this "you" and to be inconsistent in our approach. In Lecture Three we called the "you" the "first thinkable" (*primum cogitabile*, the guarantee of the world's conceivability, something that is always giving but never given, something that is believed but never objectively experienced. In Lecture Four, on the other hand, the "you" appeared to be a concrete human person; and the relations with the "you" appeared to have psychological aspects, capable of development, change and disappearance. Faith, too, in the "you " was co-motivated by the psychological and social situation of persons. This showed that faith in a concrete "you" can be shaken. The change of the "you" into "the other," into "another" and finally into "one other among many others" appeared to be perfectly plausible.

Thus a certain vacillation seems to permeate the whole of our discussion. Objections present themselves spontaneously. How can the concrete be something that is never given? How can that which is experienced be, at the same time, an object of faith? How is it possible that what is most familiar is, at the same time, mysterious? In the following pages we will attempt to answers these questions and remove the seeming contradiction.

2. Difficulties of Dialogal Philosophy

With the formulation of these objections we enter into the very heart of the problem of dialogal philosophy. The vulnerability of so-called "dialogal philosophy" lies precisely in this that the fundamental idea, the idea of the "you," is not ontologically justified. That is why they have the most diverse concepts of it. For Ferdinand Ebner the "you" is evidently God;[1] for Ludwig Binswanger it is just as evidently the

---

1. *Das Wort und die geistigen Realitäten*, Regensburg, 1921.

beloved man;[2] for Martin Buber the "you" is every being which, through a mystical experience, enters into an intimate relationship with my mind.[3] None of these three concepts, however, is very satisfactory from a philosophical standpoint. This can easily be shown.

With respect to Buber, we wholeheartedly agree that mysticism can make philosophical thinking fruitful. This is sufficiently shown by the history of philosophy from Pythagoras to Simone Weil. But this does not remove the fact that mystical experience as such is not a universal experience; consequently, it cannot constitute the foundation of an analysis that claims universal validity.

Ebner is with God from the very start and does not ask himself how others come to God. His argument is not properly philosophical. And in addition he manifests a supreme contempt for philosophy.

This leaves Binswanger. He deserves more attention than we can give him here, for his main work is rich in ideas that are valuable for us, such as his rejection of the "one-sidedly constituting intentionality,"[4] his view that the "we" is the condition which makes constitution possible,[5] and his concepts "gift," "donation," "favor" and "grace," which throw a clear light on the receptivity of the loving human being.[6]

Yet, Binswanger's attempt cannot be considered to be fully successful. It remains open to a fundamental criticism. Let us briefly indicate the reasons why we cannot rely on Binswanger here.

Binswanger's starting point lies — albeit in a negative way — in Heidegger's famous analysis of *Dasein*. Binswanger opposes Heidegger's thesis that the structure of "care" determines human existence in all its forms. He holds that "loving 'we-ness' " transcends worldliness, historicity and even finiteness.[7] Later, however, he adds that every love has its history[8] and that human love cannot exist without being contradicted by "care."[9] He finally has to confess that " love in and for itself could understand neither being nor itself . . . , for that which *makes possible* not only the understanding of being but also being-active and maintaining oneself 'in being' is the *finiteness* of care."[10] In

---

2. *Grundformen und Erkenntnis menschlichen Daseins,* Munich, 3rd. ed., 1952.
3. *Ich und Du.*
4. *Grundformen* . . . , p. 21.
5. *Ibid.,* p. 79.
6. *Ibid.,* p. 230.
7. *Ibid.,* p. 154.
8. *Ibid.,* p. 167.
9. *Ibid.,* p. 220.
10. "Liebe an und für sich nämlich könnte weder das Sein noch sich selbst verstehen . . ., denn was sowohl das Seinsverständnis als die Betätigung und Bewährung 'im Sein' *ermöglicht,* ist die *Endlichkeit* der Sorge." *Ibid.,* p. 267.

short, Binswanger is forced to recognize that in reality human love is inseparably connected with "care," that is, historicity, worldliness and finiteness belong to the essential characteristics of love, and without these love could not be active and maintain itself in being.

If this is true, the question must be asked whether a "phenomenological-anthropological demonstration"[11] should not take its starting point in man's concrete existence as it really occurs. Should not the "*Dasein*-analytical" viewpoints, such as "love in and for itself" and "care in and for itself" remain subordinate to the phenomenologist's primary task, which is faithfully to report that which appears?

There is an unintentional irony, so it appears, in the fact that Binswanger approvingly quotes a statement of the German romanticist Franz Baader who says that a supra-worldly, supra-historical and supra-existential human love is a "phantasmagory."[12] What *is* a "phantasmagory" for an unromantic phenomenologist? It is, one will answer, the imagined of my imagining, the fancied of my fancying, the imagined *noema* of my imagining *noesis*. This answer really says everything that can be said if I am a transcendental constituting Ego. But if the concept of a "one-sidedly constituting" transcendental Ego is rejected, then this answer says nothing.

The Question About the Ontological Dimension of the Dialogue

We find here a fundamental deficiency in the enterprise of dialogal philosophy. Even Michael Theunissen, a passionate protagonist of the dialogists, sees himself forced to address a serious reporach to them at the end of a series of studies of numerous dialogal authors. These thinkers, he remarks, limit themselves to showing that certain phenomena *de facto* do occur, but they fail to examine their ontological relevance.[13] Thus they avoid the answer to crucial questions. What, for example, is the ontological status of Baader's and Binswanger's "phantasmagory"? What is the philosophical significance of Ebner's experience of God? What philosophical conclusions can be drawn from Buber's extremely personal mystical experiences? All we can say is that they were *de facto* lived in a "dialogal situation," taking the term "dialogal" in the broadest sense. But the ontological significance of the dialogal event remains unclarified.

This brings us to a point where a crucial decision must be made. We have a choice to make. We could limit ourselves to playing the role of the historian of dialogal philosophy, even that of a critical historian, but we could also try to proceed in a constructive way. If we opt for

11. *Ibid.*, p. 154, note 7.
12. *Ibid.*, p. 157.
13. *Der Andere*, p. 484.

the latter, we must ask ourselves: Could it not be the task of a dialogal phenomenology to complement the work of the great dialogist in this decisive point by supplying a crucial ontological orientation?

We will try here briefly to assemble the elements needed for the introduction of the ontological dimension into dialogal philosophy. Three concepts, which have already played a role in the preceding lectures are, we think, eminently suited to serve as ontological points of orientation; they are the notions of "faith," "life" and "world." Their exact content and their interconnection must become topics of a more profound inquiry.

3. Faith

A Fundamental Human Attitude

"Faith," as we said, should not be understood exclusively or primarily as a function of religious consciousness. Similarly, for us the "content of faith" does not refer to the totality of philosophical convictions which some philosophers, such as Karl Jaspers and Gabriel Marcel, call "philosophical faith." For us "having faith," "being a believer" refers to a general human attitude.

This attitude is not even foreign to the atheist. He, too, cannot avoid having faith in certain people, regarding their statements as true, their judgments as well-grounded and their evaluations as right, although he is unable to verify them. This general human "faith" is, of course, related to the trust which the other generates in us, sometimes also with the authority which he possesses in our respect.

Nevertheless, "faith" is not the same as the uncritical and unreflecting acceptance of an opinion, a way of thinking or even a prejudice. Faith, let us say it again, is not belief in the sense David Hume gives to this term. For in any act of faith, even if it is not a religious act, something is recognized as true, affirmed as valid, and accepted with an inner conviction. In short, faith is a mode of real — and not only seeming — thetic knowing, even though it remains true that faith, like all knowing, is exposed to the danger of error. The phenomenology of this special mode of knowing has been hitherto somewhat neglected, although it is true that in published[13a] and unpublished manuscripts Husserl himself treats the themes of "faith" and "evidence of faith."

A difficulty presents itself here. The religious man and the theologian will be inclined to reserve the term "faith" for religious belief. If they are Christians they will add that faith is a wholly gratuitous "grace," a gift and that, consequently, "having faith" should not be called a human attitude and even less a general human attitude.

13a. See, e.g., *Die Krisis* . . . , pp. 335 f.

Perhaps this difficulty is not as serious as it seems. Even if with most Christian theologians one admits that saving faith is a grace, an incomprehensible and mysterious gift, one will still have to recognize that this gift is accepted or rejected by man in this world. This acceptance — or rejection — of faith appears in the formally and materially determined world; it has its anthropological, psychological, sociological and historical aspects.

The recognition of this fact does not contradict the mystery character which Christian theology ascribes to faith. But this recognition is connected with a certain view about what a mystery is. We may refer here to what we have said at the end of Lecture Three: "The mystery does not lie in a world behind the world; it does not hide behind the reality of bodies, sense data or socio-historical processes. The mystery occurs among us, near us and, to some extent, through us."[14] Nothing, therefore, prevents us from considering the mystery of faith in the present context *insofar as* it makes its appearance through us. In this way we can speak of human attitudes, situations and acts, which are the indispensable — albeit insufficient, according to most Christian theologians — conditions for faith in the religious sense.

Accordingly, there is room for a phenomenology of believing *noeses* and the corresponding believed *noemata*. But, as we said, since Husserl very little attention has been paid to this realm of phenomenological inquiry. This does not mean, of course, that philosophers did not reflect upon the peculiar character of knowing through faith. On the contrary, there exists extensive literature about this topic. From this treasury of thoughts, interpretations and analyses we have selected one treatise for special consideration. It was written by an author who has been mentioned repreatedly in the preceding pages, namely, Martin Buber.

Buber's View of the Act of Faith

Buber's remarkable study TWO WAYS OF BELIEVING takes its point of departure in "simple facts of life."[15] It is a well-known phenomenon that "I have trust in someone without being able to give a sufficient foundation for this trust." A second phenomenon is that "again without being able to assign an adequate foundation for it, I recognize something as true."[16] The fact that I am unable to indicate a sufficient reason for my attitude should not be ascribed to a lack of intelligence. What manifests itself here is an essential characteristic of my relation-

---

14. Cf. above, p. 68.
15. *Sämtliche Werke,* vol. I, p. 653.
16. *Ibid.,* p. 653.

ship to the person in whom I trust or to the judgment which I recognize as true. In neither case does the relationship arise from a reasoning process that would force me to an attitude of trust or to the recognition of a truth. True, I can subsequently indicate reasons which support my believing orientation, but these reasons are not compelling motives. This is no accident, for the act of faith, which I make with my entire self, transcends everything that could be a possible object of my thinking.

Religious faith differs from this "believing" attitude in the general sense because it refers to something which is objectively — and not only subjectively — unconditionally valid. "That means, the believing relationship here is no longer concerned with something which is in itself conditioned and only for me an unconditioned 'someone' or 'something,' but with something which is also in itself unconditioned.[17] Religious faith also appears in two essentially different forms: one can believe in *someone* and one can believe in *something*.

Next, Buber tries to demonstrate at some length that the first way of believing was characteristic of the people of Israel in its early history and that the second way is typical of primitive Christianity. We will omit here Buber's exegetic and historical investigations, which constitute the major part of the above mentioned work,[18] and simply address his fundamental idea.

Is it phenomenologically speaking, right to say that the act of "believing" can be brought about in two different ways, viz., as the trust I give *someone* and as the trust I place in *something*? We are inclined to recognize the correctness of Buber's view, but we would primarily draw our arguments from non-religious everyday experience.

In everyday life it is commonplace to trust the truth of an announcement, the justice of a legal regulation, the reliability of a technical product, without being able to justify our spontaneous trust through proofs. It also happens to us that we "believe" in someone. Of course, we do not trust him blindly. Usually, the person's competency, loyalty and reliability have repreatedly manifested themselves. But this fact is not yet a reason why we should "believe" in this person. "To believe," says Buber, "is to persevere in trust";[19] and it is precisely for this perseverance in our trust that we cannot put forward any compelling motives. What reveals itself here is a kind of surrender of our person to the trustworthy person of the other.

---

17. "Das heiszt, das Glaubensverhältnis ist hier nicht mehr eines zu einem an sich bedingten, nur für mich unbedingten 'Jemand' oder 'Sachverhalt', sondern einem auch an sich unbedingtem." *Ibid.,* p. 654.
18. *Ibid.,* pp. 654-786.
19. *Ibid.,* p. 655.

Complement of Buber's Thesis

Buber's study is an important contribution to the phenomenology of believing. But, we may ask, is it satisfactory from a philosophical standpoint? Strictly speaking, Buber limits himself to the observation of an exegetic and religious-historical fact: there are two ways of believing, one which is found in the early history of Israel and the other among the first Christians and in the Apostle Paul. Perhaps it will happen in the future, Buber adds at the end of his treatise, that the representatives of the typically Jewish belief in God and those of the typically Christian belief will better understand each other and help each others in ways that we today can barely imagine. But this mutual understanding does not remove the fact that believing in someone and believing in something are and will remain "essentially different."[20]

For the philosopher this cannot be the last word. For, if there is such an abyss between these two human attitudes, why do we call both of them "believing" attitudes? If both attitudes are forms of "believing," in spite of all their differences, then this common essence must be the topic of a question. Moreover, a search should be made for the ontological foundation of this agreement, which is not just fortuitous. If this search is omitted, we deserve the reproach, addressed by Michael Theunissen to the dialogists, that they usually are satisfied with drawing attention to phenomena but neglect to inquire about their ontological significance.

Let us, therefore, approach the problem from the phenomenological standpoint. We will start with concrete cases, limiting ourselves at first to instances in which the content of a certain communication is or is not believed. Let us, then, analyze our attitude in the following three situations:

1. The local newspaper carries an official report from the civil registry that yesterday the 250,000th inhabitant of the city was born at the municipal hospital.

2. The newspapers of a country at war report a series of military successes. The enemy suffered heavy losses; our troups had no lethal casualties.

3. Someone tells me that he loves me.

In all three cases it should be evident that, in the evaluation of the truth of the communication, the decisive factor does not primarily lie in a critique of the logical or linguistic form of the communication but in the evaluation of the person from whom the message originates. Nevertheless, there is a difference. In the first two cases the evaluation of the person or persons who make the communication also takes into

---

20. *Ibid.,* p. 782.

account the communicator's situation. Their experience, knowledge of man, prescientific or scientific understanding of typical situations play an important role in the formation of the judgment.

Let us illustrate this point by means of our examples. The civil registry office, so I will think in the first case, has no serious reasons to issue a false report about the number of people living in the city. In the past, moreover, I have received certain impressions showing that the officials are competent and reliable. I therefore "believe" the announcement of the 250,000th inhabitant. With respect to nations at war, on the other hand, I know from past experience that their situation often forces them to announce military successes. I am familiar also with the stereotype schema of such war communications. For this reason I do not believe the newspapers' announcement of glorious victories.

In all this there is no question of evidence. It is not to be excluded that the civil authorities, so reliable in the past, did lie this time. On the other hand, it is conceivable that the war information office for once did not indulge in propaganda but simply announced the truth. I am aware of these concrete possibilities when I say "I believe" or "I don't believe." By believing or not believing, I make a certain decision and accept certain risks. But in the two above-mentioned cases there is a "calculated risk." By virtue of the data I have in my objectifying experience, the proper aspect of belief — or unbelief, for unbelief is also a belief — is reduced to a minimum.

The situation is different in the third case. If I have any experience and knowledge of men, I can, of course, try to compare my situation with other situations in which one human being tells another: "I love you." Probably I will be inclined to make such comparisons. And I will then take into account the age, sex, the social, cultural and historical conditions of the persons concerned. But the results of my comparison will be disappointing. For, if I know people, I know also that age, sex, social, cultural and historical conditions can be exactly the same and that, in spite of this, the declaration of love of the one can be wholly trustworthy and that of the other absolutely incredible.

How can this difference be explained? Apparently by the fact that all data, all circumstances, even the entire surrounding world are colored by the character of the loving other person. Buber's words, "Everything else lives in *his* light,"[21] i.e., the light of the other, are appropriate here. Thus my attempts to determine the other's being with the aid of the being of the surrounding world produce very little result.

---

21. *Ich und Du,* p. 83.

This is not all, however. The very words of the "communication" have a different meaning as spoken by this person rather than someone else. No logical, syntactical or semantic analysis can remove this fundamental ambiguity. For the words, "I love you," are not a communication in the proper sense of the term. A comparison with the first two cases shows this. The child of which the first case spoke was born or not born, independently of the question whether its birth was officially announced or not. The military victory was obtained or the defeat suffered; the newspapers' triumphant announcement does not change the reality in the least. But what is predicated in the third case does not exist independently of the one who predicates it and is not independent of the act of predicating. Buber, therefore, is right when he emphasizes that there is no question here of a "objective fact" (*Sachverhalt*).

The question whether or not I attach credence to the last-named communication, unsurprisingly, depends almost exclusively on my relationship with the other who "communicates," that is, "shares himself" with me. For, let us repeat it, my objectifying experience is of little use here. On the contrary, the decisive element is the other's personal being in relationship with my personal being. In my decision I am thrown back upon myself and there is no longer any question of a "calculated risk." Just the opposite is the case. If I believe in the other's love and open myself to it, my risk is total; and if, on the other hand, I do not believe in that love and reject the other, the danger for my existence is just as great. The rule that applies to the dialogal relationship appears to be: if I believe, I wholly surrender to the other in whom I believe; if I do not believe, I totally close myself to the other in whom I do not believe; and both attitudes imply a risk that is total.

The Primacy of Faith in the Person

Our analysis shows that there are indeed great differences in the "believing" attitudes of man. In the first two cases the act of "believing" was supported and guided by a maximum of objective knowledge, but in the third case objective data played only a very minor role. At the same time, however, the analysis shows that the three acts of "belief" have something in common. This common essence could be expressed in the following way. The question whether or not we will believe the content of a communication depends on the preliminary question whether or not we believe in the one who makes the communication. Differently expressed, we only believe something if it comes from someone in whom we believe. In every case belief in the person precedes belief in the statements made by that person.

This essential law may not — at least not primarily — be conceived as a psychological rule. Rather, it expresses an ontological insight. The correctness of this law is apparent from its connection with the results of our preceding investigations. If it is true that the "you" is always older than the "I," if the original relationship between "me" and the "you" is a relationship of faith, then we are dealing here with an original ontological relationship. Phenomenologically this relationship could be characterized as: "I believe in you because you are who you are." It is in this that the essence of the fundamental I-you-relationship consists.

From this it follows, next, that I, the believer, will not close myself to that in which you indirectly manifest yourself. In reference to the phenomenology of knowledge this means that, if I have faith in you, I'll also recognize as true the communications coming from you. Differently expressed, I believe your word because you are worthy of belief. Note that this formula cannot be reversed. No flood of words, no eloquence, no clever arguments and no massive propaganda efforts could ever induce me to believe in you as a person. They would merely serve to confirm me in my attitude of rejection and unbelief with respect to your word. Faith in the person appears to have primacy here.

The conclusion to be drawn from this is simple but important. It confirms the fundamental ideas expressed in the preceding lectures. The I-you-relationship is more original than the I-it-relationship. This is the profound reason why faith in a "you" precedes my belief in a "communication" coming from this "you." Thus the psychology of belief — or unbelief, respectively — rests upon an ontological structure. This structure, in its turn, is connected with the finiteness of the person and his ontological dependence on the other.[22] There is no need to insist again on this point.

The Role of Objectification

The two ways of believing sketched above are forms of knowledge. From the viewpoint of the genesis of awareness they should even be considered to be the oldest forms of knowledge. They are, as we saw in Lecture Four, the conditions from which knowledge of objects and objective relations can arise. This, however, does not remove the fact that belief, based on feeling, is something primitive and must be overcome. Understanding the nature of things, the cause and effect relationship or that of end and means belongs to the humanization of man. As man matures, therefore, critical, objectifying knowledge will constitute the dialectical antithesis of primitive belief, based on feeling.[23] In this sense the antithesis of objectification cannot be dis-

22. Cf. above, pp. 107 f.
23. Cf. above, pp. 91 ff.

pensed with in the maturation of man and man's world-view. But this same antithesis is also necessary if man is to arrive at faith in the proper sense of the term. This point must now be discussed.

What do we mean by "faith in the proper sense"? It refers, as we saw,[24] to an affirmation of reality which in its inmost essence is independent of objectifying knowledge. This provisional description demands further explanation. Let us add, therefore, that the description contains the implicit thesis that one who believes, in the proper sense, must already have at his disposal objectifying knowledge, knowledge that is based on experience and reflection, but his believing affirmation transcends the limits of what can be adequately experienced as an object and reflected upon. In other words, the genuine affirmation of faith goes beyond anything that can be adequately given as an object of experience and of thought.

From this seemingly simple observation three conclusions must be drawn. First, even the most authentic act of faith does not occur, as it were, in a vacuum. It always demands something concrete, which is the object of experience and reflection and which in the first instance makes the "leap of faith" possible. This something can be a person, a community, a tradition, an action, symbol or writing. These concrete realities function as the spring-board for the act of faith in the proper sense.

Because we do not wish to enter here the realm of philosophy of religion, we prefer to use an example borrowed from profane experience. When I "believe" in the faithfulness of a friend, the obvious implication is that I have already a certain knowledge of him. But my assertion of "belief" in him goes beyond the data of experience. I transcend all the facts known to me and give expression to my conviction that, no matter what situations will arise, my friend's faithfulness to me will prove to be unshakeable.

Belief in the faithfulness of a friend, therefore, presupposes knowledge of social life and interhuman relations. Yet, in the midst of these concrete data there is something which cannot be shown as such and which I can only seize in an act of faith.

Jaspers compares a concrete datum that can give access to transcendence to a sign in a secret alphabet, a "cipher." As he tells us in his METAPHYSICS, it is not the metaphysical hypothesis treated by my reflection that shows Being to me, but "the bodily presence of the cipher, beyond which I do not think, because Being shines in it."[25] Let us interpret these words in the light of our own ideas. "Bodily

---

24. Cf. above, p. 123.
25. "... die Leibhaftigkeit der Chiffre, über die ich nicht hinausdenke, weil in ihr das Sein leuchtet." *Philosophie,* vol. III, *Metaphysik,* Berlin, 1932, p. 131.

present" to me is a "you," as we have said; and what Being is becomes clear to me only when I have encountered a being that "is" as I "am."

The first of all secret signs, then, for me is a concrete "you." But this "you" is not that secret sign which gives access to transcendence, insofar as this "you" can be experienced and become the starting point of logical deductions. Rather, something can become accessible to me thanks to the "you" and in the "you, something which I can only understand as a "believer. In Jaspers' terminology, the "you" is a cipher which can only be "read" in an attitude of faith.

Secondly, it should be obvious that my mode of transcendence is not wholly independent from the course of my experience. The "springboard" determines the direction of the leap. Let us illustrate this by a concrete example. The way a child experiences his parents can be decisive for his religious development. As Adolf Busemann writes, "The unconditional love of the parents lays the foundation in a feeling of being-sheltered, of elementary security. This original shelteredness is at the same time the original model and 'pre-school' of all later trust and therefore also of one's being-sheltered in God."[26]

Thirdly — and this is forgotten by many writers — the moment can come when a particular concrete experience appears no longer suitable to serve as a "spring-board" for my faith. In Jaspers' language, a certain "cipher" then appears no longer as legible. This idea applies also to the particular "cipher" which a concrete "you" was for me. It should even be considered normal and inevitable that at a given stage in my development a "you" in which I believed becomes for me "unbelievable." For otherwise I would always remain a serf of the first concrete "you" that I encountered in my life. My life would then be stifled and my development would be fixed at a certain stage. Such a fixation should not be considered to be the normal course of affairs.

It goes without saying that the discovery of the insufficiency of a particular "you" can be very disappointing to me; it can make me bitter and give rise to discouragement. An old form of faith perishes, and this is always a painful experience for one who believed. At the same time, however, this is also a condition for the birth of new and more mature forms of faith; it is what keeps faith alive.

4. Life and World

In this way we arrive at the second of our three fundamental con-

---

26. "Die bedingungslose Liebe der Eltern legt die Grundlage im Gefühl der Geborgenheit, einer elementaren Sicherheit. Diese Urgeborgenheit ist zugleich die Urform und Vorschule alles späteren Vertrauens und so auch der Geborgenheit in Gott." *Geborgenheit und Entwurzelung des jungen Menschen,* Ratingen, 2nd ed., 1955, p. 28.

cepts, viz., life. Unlike most philosophers who write about life, we do not see life as a stream that uninterruptedly flows in the same direction, not as an *élan* directed to one and the same end, or as the continuous succession of constituting achievements aiming at the same end.

From the phenomenological standpoint it should be emphasized that what is given in the first place is not life as such, identical and uniform, but a plurality of living beings, divergent forms of life and different poles of life. To these beings Heraclitus' saying that war is the father of all things seems to apply: life conquers life, life devours life, life feeds on life. Yet, this saying should not be interpreted exclusively in the sense of a struggle for life among organisms. On a spiritual level the same essential law of life manifests itself in a different way. The rule here is that a higher form of life does not arise unless the lower form is somehow overcome; and this does not happen without effort, struggle, pain, crisis and anxiety. To this level of life also, therefore, Heraclitus' remark about the creative character of struggle is applicable.

Summarizing, we can say that life in all its finite forms is construction and destruction, coming to be and passing away, victory and, at the same time, defeat. The philosopher should take these phenomena into account. He should realize that life without drama, tragedy even, is inconceivable. This, let us repeat, applies to all forms of life, even the life of faith, as we have seen. And this idea holds also for the world-constituting life of a "we."

World

Just as faith, in the above-described phenomenological sense, is a normal function of my human life, and the "you" is that which normally is first believed, so also a world is that which normally is constituted in the dialogue between an "I" and a "you." For a formally and materially determined world is, as we have seen, nothing but the orderly whole of objects which I, thanks to my dialogue with a "you," constitute.[27] In the light of the preceding considerations, however, this assertion needs to be expressed in a more differentiated way. The world-constituting dialogue derives its constituting power from my belief in a concrete "you." Because I have faith in a "you," I am also convinced that the objects which this "you" puts forward in his dialogue with me are real. This shows that the dialogue proceeds in a normal fashion only as long as I consider my partner in the dialogue worthy of belief.

---

27. Cf. above, pp. 65 ff.

As soon as I begin to doubt his trustworthiness, a significant change occurs. In Husserl's terminology, this change may be characterized as follows. The "you" in question, which was a subject of "our" world, becomes an object in "my" world. In the language of Marcel, the "you" with whom I conversed becomes a "he," a "she" or an "it" about which I speak. With whom do I speak about it? With another "you," of course. For the basis of my entire change lies in the encounter with a new "you," one which evokes more confidence in me than my former partner who has now become untrustworthy.

Let us illustrate the matter by an example which is more or less connected with Lecture Four. There comes a moment in the life of a boy when he no longer believes in a magical explanation of the world. What Granny told him about Santa Claus, Father Christmas and the Easter Bunny becomes a fairy tale for him. He now swears by the authority of his teacher and the latter's knowledge of science and technology. Granny's authority is undermined; she is no longer a trustworthy partner in a dialogue. He describes her to his teacher as a superstitious and ignorant old woman. On the basis of his elementary scientific way of looking at things, the boy now constitutes a different world than the world he believed in when he was younger and was convinced that magical forces and powers rule the universe.

Sooner or later, of course, the boy will also discover that the teacher does not know everything, that there are gaps in his knowledge and that his scientific explanations are incomplete, superficial and unsatisfactory. But this might well be only the beginning of a more radical change of attitude. In his late teens when he goes to a college or university, he may come to understand that the systematic increase in knowledge is no guarantee of progress, that greater technological control over nature does not necessarily mean more social justice, and that modern rapid communication does not automatically foster world peace. Our student now no longer believes in instructors and professors who expect salvation from science. He looks upon his professors as autoritarian, narrow-minded and decrepit figures. He now believes in a senior fellow-student and the latter's political slogans. Once again, he lives in an "entirely different world."

This brief description may suffice to clarify the following important conclusion: the birth and disappearance of forms of faith exercise influence on the world of the "believer." If his life takes a turn which upsets his "rocklike convictions," his world also assumes a different character. What formerly was a simple and comprehensible complex of beings now seems unclear, uncertain and ambiguous. Matters may go so far that ultimately he sees himself obliged to relativize the whole of beings which formerly were real for him and place them "between brackets." This is what we have called the "reduction."[28]

The affair does not end with this, however. For a crisis is always a state of transition. By means of new dialogues, the person in crisis will constitute a new world. This new world will share some of the characteristics of the old one because total discontinuity is inconceivable, but in other respects it will be different.

In this way man's world develops together with man himself. And what has been said above with respect to the individual applies also to groups of people, nations and civilizations. A higher civilization. for instance, can play the role of a concrete "you" in reference to a lower civilization. Accordingly, the ideas of dialogal phenomenology can serve as the philosophical foundation of empirical anthropology, developmental psychology, social psychology and cultural psychology.

5. *The Importance of a Dynamic View of the I-You Relationship*

For philosophy itself something else is important, namely, the fact that the I-you relationship is conceived here in a thoroughly dynamic fashion. This safeguards us against the mistake which dialogal philosophers have not always avoided. By making the terms "I" and "you" always refer to the same fixed and unchangeable poles of reality, they, too, lapse into a kind of solipsism. For the one subject-pole they substitute two such poles, but the abyss between this bi-unity and its objects remains unbridgeable. It then remains an enigma how, in Buber's language, the "you" can ever become an "it" and, reversely, and "it" a "you," or, using Theunissen's terminology, how the "you" can "change." In such a case dialogal philosophy would exclude any social philosophy; it would become a "double-headed solipsism." Herein lies the importance of a philosophical approach which does not exclude but includes development, life, change, conflict, crisis and renewal.

You and World

Some dialogal philosophers speak as if the "you" is the perfect counterpart of the entire worldly reality, but their statements in this matter lack clarity. It will be possible, we think, to contribute to the clarification of this question by more carefully distinguishing the various concepts of "world." The answer to the question may perhaps be different according as we use the horizon concept of the world or that of a materially and formally determined world.[29] With respect to the former, it should be evident that I can encounter a "you" only with-

---

28. Cf. above, p. 96.
29. Cf. above, pp. 24 ff.

in the universal horizon which unites all beings into a single whole. We may add that it is precisely this original unity that makes an encounter with a "you" possible.

"The 'you' does not come into the world," we said, but it is already in the world."[30] Negatively, this means that the "you" is not in a "celestial place" (*topos uranios*) separated from the world or in an "intelligible world" (*mundus intelligibilis*). It is not a Platonic idea, not a Kantian *noumenon*, not a Husserlian *eidos*. The "you" is concrete; I actually encounter it; I encounter it here and now or I never encounter it at all.

The "you," then, is in the world. But this does not at all mean that the "you" is a datum for me. The "you" is not one of the many objects of which a materially and formally determined world is composed for me. More accurately expressed, insofar as the "you" is fully "you," you are not for me a datum to which I am orientated in an objectifying way, that is, by judging, evaluating and willing.

Why is the "you" never simply something given for me? In the preceding considerations we have seen several reasons: the "you" is always older than the "I"; you are the co-constituting subject and not a constituted object; it is free and therefore not fully objectifiable. We must add now a fourth reason, which is the most important of all — namely, the "you" is not a datum for me because I believe in it.

Let us be more precise. The other is, of course, also a concrete datum of experience; but the other can become a "you." What I have experienced with respect to the other merely serves me as a spring-board enabling me to believe in something that is no longer "given." In other words, I transcend everything in the other that can be experienced and in this way I am enabled to reach the dimension of the "you" in whom I believe.

The answer, then, that I will have to give to the typically phenomenological question, "How does the 'you' appear?" is, "The 'you' appears to me; it appears to me in the world, but as veiled by something which is not the 'you'." I see the "you," but I see it only in likenesses. Through the transcending movement of my mind I grasp something of the "you," but what I grasp reveals itself only as a fragment, an aspect of the "you." In short, the "you" is not a datum for me but a task. I seek it as long as I live, and I seek it in the others. For the others appear to me as "ciphers," in which, as I believingly assume, the mystery of the other is written.

It is from this original situation that flows the dialectic of the encounter. An encounter is, of course, not an accidental "bumping"

---

30. Cf. above, pp. 51 f.

into each other of two subjects. But the opposite is equally unthinkable; that is, the encounter must not be conceived as a "fate" which decides my lot without me. The encounter has a dialectic character. This is a point which has hitherto not be sufficiently understood.

Let us present a typical schema of the nature of that dialectic. We will see that it normally passes through certain phases, which may perhaps be designated by the terms "belief," "unbelief" and "believing recognition." We insist upon the term "schema," to indicate that we do not wish to sketch here an outline of psychological development. All this schema amounts to is a modest sample of what one could perhaps call a "metaphysical reflection upon the course of human life."

Dialectic of My Encounter

The first "you" is with me before I am with myself. I do not choose that "you" in any way. It is Mother.

Mother is gentle. She gives herself completely to me; with her I know that I am securely sheltered.

I cannot avoid believing that Mother is the "you" for me. She gives me everything I need to live, grow and change.

When I have grown and changed, I encounter Father. Father knows the great world. He has experience, daring, the spirit of enterprise. He frees powers in me. Mother is different; she cannot do that.

I no longer believe in Mother. Mother is a worrysome, unexperienced, narrow-minded woman. She is a woman like so many other women.

I believe with a rock-fast faith that Father is the "you." He gives me whatever I need to live and grow and change.

When I have grown and changed, I encounter the Friend. He has youthful dash, esprit and originality. He opens new perspectives to me. He makes me see an intellectual landscape that was entirely unknown to me. Father is not like him; he cannot do it. Father is blind to all those fascinating new things.

I no longer believe in Father. Father is an old-fashioned authoritarian. He is a man like many other men.

This is the way my life runs its course. The "you's" change and every "you" is a station on my road. My voyage, so it seems, is an idle wandering without a goal. Yet my journey is not in vain. The longer it lasts, the better I see that every "you" that I have encountered does indeed reflect something of *the* "you" which I seek and continue to seek. This realization is the bitter fruit of my many errors.

Afterwards, when it is too late, I realize that Mother made me truly see something of *the* "you" by the fact that she was gentle, gave herself and drove away my anxieties.

Afterwards, when it is too late, I realize that Father truly made me see something of *the* "you" by the fact that he unleashed new powers in me.

Afterwards, when it is too late, I realize that the Friend truly personified something of the "you" for me when he opened a new perspective for me.

Afterwards, I know ever more. I know then that my passionate affirmations of yesteryear were just as naive as my passionate negations. I then realize that to "believe" is something else and something more than a "naive affirmation" or a "naive negation." My youthful affirmations and negations terminate in something new — in believing recognition. In an act by which I transcend my entire experience of life I realize that all my "you's" were road-signs and mile-posts on the road toward *the* "You."

6. Conclusions

Faithfulness

Perhaps we are justified in assigning the name "faithfulness" to the fundamental attitude of man, which consists in this that, in spite of all changes, revolutions, metamorphoses, disappointments, disillusions and crises, he continues to believe in an other. In this sense I remain faithful to *the* 'You." I continue to search for it and try to construct an image of this "You" from the most noble elements I have seen in the many "you's" I have encountered. Why I continue to seek this "You" I do not understand; my faithfulness remains incomprehensible to myself. It is part of the facticity of my existence.

The Question About the Existence of the "You"

Does *the* "You" exist? Has it always existed? Has it chosen me before all ages and does it remain faithful to me, once it has chosen me? Is my incomprehensible faithfulness an answer to its faithfulness? Is my actual fidelity the most free attitude of mind of which, thanks to my finite freedom, I am capable? Is my finite freedom destined to encounter *the* "You"?

No scientific answer can be given to such a question. Nor can any philosophical answer be thought of. Only the believer knows what to say.

But for the philosopher one thing is certain, viz., the question itself: IF THE "YOU" DOES NOT EXIST, WHY DO I CONTINUE TO SEEK IT?

INDEX OF NAMES

INDEX OF SUBJECT MATTER

136